MAKING A MODERN STREET

AN URBAN PROPOSAL – THE WORK OF 8 IRISH ARCHITECTS

BAU EINER MODERNEN STRAßE

EIN STÄDTEBAU ENTWURF – DIE ARBEIT VON 8 IRISCHEN ARCHITEKTEN

MAKING A MODERN STREET

Published to coincide with the international touring exhibition of the same name opening at the Architektur Forum Zürich in June 1991.

ISBN   0946641 196

Editors   Group 91

Design   John O'Regan

Cover   Model at scale 1:20 by Jens Küchenmeister

Photography   John Searle (models), Gerry Hayden
                (drawings), Tony Higgins (group)
Translation   Cornelia Bernegger, Marianne O'Regan
Inputting   Patricia Ormond, Marianne O'Regan
Typography   John O'Regan (typeface: Franklin Gothic)
Typesetting   Gandon Bookwork
Outputting   Type Bureau, Dublin
Printing   Beta Print, Dublin

Distributed by Gandon Distribution, Dublin (01-767101) and its overseas agents: Central Books, London (UK); Idea Books, Amsterdam (Europe); Irish Books & Media Inc (USA).

Published by Gandon Books, an imprint of Gandon Editions
GANDON EDITIONS, 15 Earlsfort Terrace, Dublin 2 (767101)

PROJECT – *Making a Modern Street* is a project for Dublin 1991 – European City of Culture. The project was initiated by Shelley McNamara and supported from its inception by both the Dublin 1991 Committee and Dublin Corporation, who made available a site in the Liberties. New PMPA sponsored the building of the models and the Dublin exhibition.

Group 91 are pleased to acknowledge the significant contributions made to the project by the following individuals:
– Dublin 1991: Lewis Clohessy and his Board, and
  Paula McDermott
– Dublin Corporation: Senator Eoin Ryan and
  Patrick Morrissey, Assistant City Manager
– New Ireland Project Managers Ltd: Joan O'Connor
– New PMPA: Jim Quigley, Ian Maguire and Rita O'Reilly
– Jens Küchenmeister Modelmakers: Jens Küchenmeister,
  David O'Brien, Maeve Gardner, Grant Abramian, and
  Barbara Küchenmeister
– Mal Stevenson

EXHIBITION – This exhibition was initiated by Norbert De Biasio of the Architektur Forum Zürich and co-ordinated in Dublin by O'Donnell and Tuomey for Group 91. The exhibition is presented in Zürich by the Cultural Relations Committee, Department of Foreign Affairs, Dublin, Ireland, and the Architektur Forum Zürich. The Architektur Forum Zürich is sponsored by the following firms: Geberit, Laufen Keramik AG, Marti Unternehmungen, Eternit, Otis.

Dublin – Riverrun Gallery – May 3 - May 18 1991
Zürich – Architektur Forum – June 13 - July 17 1991

BAU EINER MODERNEN STRAßE

© Gandon Books, 1991. Urheberrechte für die Illustrationen und Texte ist den einzelnen Architekten oder Autoren vorbehalten. Design und Buchdruker Urheberrechte: John O'Regan. Alle Rechte vorbehalten.

Dieser Katalog ist im Zusammenhang mit der gleichnamigen Ausstellung im Architektur Forum Zürich entstanden, die im Juni 1991 eröffnetwird.

ISBN   0946641 196

Herausgeber   Group 91

Entwurf   John O'Regan
Einband   Modell im Verhältnis 1:20 von
                Jens Kuchermeister
Fotografie   John Searle (Modelle), Gerry Hayden
                (Zeichnungen), Tony Higgins (Gruppe)
Übersetzung   Cornelia Bernegger, Marianne O'Regan
Eingabe   Patricia Ormond, Marianne O'Regan
Typografie   John O'Regan (Schrift: Franklin Gotisch)
Satz   Gandon Bookwork
Produktion   Type Bureau, Dublin
Druck   Beta Print, Dublin

Vertrieben von Gandon Distribution, Dublin (01-767101) und seinen Agenten in Ubersee: Central Books, London (UK); Idea Books, Amsterdam (Europe); Irish Books & Media Inc (USA).

Herausgegeben von Gandon Books, ein Druckervermerk von
GANDON EDITIONS, 15 Earlsfort Terrace, Dublin 2 (767101)

PROJEKT – Der *Bau einer modernen Straße* ist ein Projekt für Dublin 1991 – Europäische Kulturstadt. Das Projekt wurde von Shelley McNamara ins Leben gerufen und von Anfang an von sowohl dem Dublin 1991 Kommittee, als auch von den Dubliner Stadtbehörden, die das Grundstück in den Liberties zur Verfügung stellten, voll unterstützt. Die 'New PMPA' (Versicherungs) gesellschaft förderte den Bau der Modelle und die Ausstellung in Dublin.

Group 91 nehmen mit Freude die bedeutenden Beiträge zu dem Projekt von den folgenden Personen zur Kenntnis:
– Dublin 1991: Lewis Clohessy und sein Amt, und
  Paula McDermott
– Dublin Corporation: Senator Eoin Ryan und
  Patrick Morrissey, Stadtdirektorassistent
– New Ireland Project Managers Ltd: Joan O'Connor
– New PMPA: Jim Quigley, Ian Maguire und Rita O'Reilly
– Jens Küchenmeister Modelmakers: Jens Küchenmeister,
  David O'Brien, Maeve Gardner, Grant Abramian, und
  Barbara Küchenmeister
– Mal Stevenson

AUSTELLUNG – Diese Austellungwurde von Norbert de Biasio vom Architektur Forum Zürich ins Leben gerufen und in Dublin von O'Donnell and Tuomey für die Group 91 koordiniert. Die Austellung wird in Zurich von Kommittee für kulturelle Beziehungen präsentiert und vom Außen ministerium in Dublin, Irland und dem Architektur Forum in Zürich. Das Architektur Forum Zürich wird von folgenden Firmen unterstützt: Geberit, Laufen Keramik AG, Marti Unternehmungen, Eternit, Otis.

Dublin – Riverrun Gallery – Mai 3 - Mai 18 1991
Zürich – Architektur Forum – Juni 13 - Juli 17 1991

ARCHITEKTUR FORUM ZÜRICH

MAKING A MODERN STREET

AN URBAN PROPOSAL – THE WORK OF 8 IRISH ARCHITECTS

BAU EINER MODERNEN STRAßE

EIN STÄDTEBAU ENTWURF – DIE ARBEIT VON 8 IRISCHEN ARCHITEKTEN

FOREWORD

VORWORT

For myself, I always write about Dublin, because if I can get to the heart of Dublin I can get to the heart of all the cities in the world. In the particular is contained the universal. — James Joyce

Dublin has become a suburban city. The tradition of living in the city has been interrupted. In *Saving the City* Frank McDonald reminds us that 'In 1926, when it was a compact sort of place, nearly two-thirds of Dubliners lived in what we now call the inner city – the 4,000 acres or so locked in between the Grand Canal, the Royal Canal and the North Circular Road. Now it is fewer than one in twelve. Indeed, over the past 25 years, the population of the city's historic core has been cut in half – from 160,000 to just 80,000... The heart of Dublin has been almost stripped bare of the population that once sustained it.'

A generation ago, Dublin was still one of the great European cities, standing alongside Venice, Rome, Amsterdam and Bath as a supreme example of the city as a corporate work of art, one of Europe's great monuments to urban civilisation. The design and grandeur of its public buildings, the nobility of its town plan – with its squares, riverside terraces and generous streets – made it a city second to none. These remain as mere fragments, and official and popular disregard for the historic fabric of the city have long threatened to destroy utterly the character of Dublin.

To Joyce, the city of Dublin and its people were an obsession. He went to great lengths to record them with total accuracy. He frequently wrote asking for exact information concerning places that he was about to describe while writing *Ulysses*. In exile, he prided himself on his ability to "name the shops from Amiens Street to the Pillar, first one side, then the other." Yet, just as he transformed his Dublin into the world in microcosm – and, in so doing, confirmed as an epic city, as a world city of culture, not so much Dublin, perhaps, as the idea of Dublin – so, too, must we confront the greatest cultural task that Dublin now faces.

We must accept our city's rules and its forms. We must honour its history. We must cherish its memories and nourish its dreams. We must make Dublin once again a home for its scattered population, a place to be inhabited, a place to be loved. We must accept the past before we can build the future. Hence, the imperative simultaneously to explore, research and interpret that unappreciated heritage.

Was mich betrifft, so schreibe ich stets über Dublin, weil, wenn ich zum Herzen Dublins vordringe, kenne ich das Wesen aller Städte. Im Besonderen ist das Universale enthalten. — James Joyce

Dublin ist eine Vorstadt geworden. Die Tradition urbanen Wohnens wurde gestört. In seinem Buch *Rettung der Stadt* erinnert uns Frank McDonald daran, daß 1926, als Dublin noch ein kompakter Ort war, nahezu zwei Drittel der Dubliner Bevölkerung in jenem Stadtteil wohnte, den wir heute Innenstadt nennen – ungefähr 16 qkm, die zwischen dem Grand Canal, dem Royal Canal und der North Circular Road eingeschlossen sind. Heute ist es nur noch gerade ein Zwölftel. In der Tat ist die Bevölkerung der Dubliner Altstadt in den letzten 25 Jahren auf die Hälfte geschrumpft, von 160.000 auf nur noch 80.000... Das Herz von Dublin hat sich der Bewohner entledigt, die die Stadt einst ausmachten.

Eine Generation früher war Dublin noch eine der großen europäischen Metropolen neben Venedig, Rom, Amsterdam und Bath als ein herausragendes Beispiel einer Stadt, als Gesamtkunstwerk, eines der großen europäischen Monumente der urbanen Zivilisation. Die Gestalt und Grandeur seiner öffentlichen Gebäude, die Vornehmheit des Stadtbildes – mit seinen Plätzen, seinen Uferpromenaden und seinen großzügigen Straßen – machte es zu einer Stadt ohne ihresgleichen. Es bleiben davon bloß Fragmente, und die Gleichgültigkeit von Behörden und Bevölkerung gegenüber dem historisch gewachsenen Stadtgefüge drohen schon lange den Charakter Dublins vollends zu zerstören.

Für Joyce waren Dublin und dessen Bewohner eine Obsession. Er holte weit aus, um sie mit absoluter Präzision wiedergeben zu können. Während er an *Ulysses* schrieb, holte er oft genaue Erkundigungen über Plätze ein, mit deren Beschreibung er sich gerade befaßte. Im Exil rühmte er sich seiner Fähigkeit, 'alle Läden von der Amiens Street bis zur Säule beim Namen nennen zu können, zuerst die eine, dann die andere Seite'. Doch genauso, wie er sein Dublin in eine Welt im Mikrokosmos verwandelte – und, indem er das tat, bestätigte er sie als eine epische Stadt, als eine Weltstadt der Kultur, nicht so sehr Dublin selbst, vielleicht, als die Idee dieser Stadt – so müssen auch wir der größten kulturellen Aufgabe, die sich Dublin heute stellt, entgegentreten.

Wir müssen die Gesetze unserer Stadt und ihre Formen akzeptieren. Wir müssen ihre Geschichte würdigen. Wir müssen ihre Erinnerungen pflegen und ihre Träume nähren.

Group 91 have staked a powerful claim for Dublin as a European city, renouncing through the counterprojects of the 1980s the notion of Dublin as a car-centred American-style city. The proposals for Bachelor's Walk rejected comprehensive redevelopment as a means of rejuvenating the inner city. And, under the banner of the City Architecture Studio, the redevelopment of Dublin's docklands was foreseen years before officialdom recognised its potential. Group 91 share a deep conviction about urban architecture and an optimism about the future of Dublin as it faces into a new millennium. Fundamental to our work is the thesis that urban design and the interpretation of the city is enriched by the interaction of varied viewpoints within an overall consensus. That is why we work together. We believe that architects who share a common ground should come together to consolidate that ground, to develop a cohesive architectural praxis of the highest quality and to bring about change.

Making a Modern Street seeks to reinterpret the traditional Dublin urban house and to bring to a range of new urban house types, which could be used to repair the fabric of the inner city, the qualities offered by the Georgian terrace. The intention is to have an exhibition of buildings, to build a modern residential street – to remake the street and re-establish the primacy of the public realm. The chosen site, on the corner of Meath Street and South Earl Street in the Liberties, lies derelict today. But in 1866, on the very same site, the Industrial Tenements Society built four-storey tenement blocks, designed by Charles Geoghegan – the first philanthropic society housing to be built in Dublin. Now the site of that radical, nineteenth-century housing prototype is to serve as the birthplace of several new urban housing prototypes to suit our contemporary social and economic structures. So much has changed during the intervening years, and yet so much remains the same. We still need to improve the quality of life of our citizens. And the most important weapon in our armoury is to create once more a living city, a socially mixed city. That is the vision behind *Making a Modern Street*.

– Shane O'Toole

O'Connell Street, Dublin, 1900

Wir müssen Dublin einmal mehr zu einem Zuhause für seine verstreute Bevölkerung machen, zu einem Ort, der bewohnt werden soll, zu einem Ort, der geliebt werden soll. Wir müssen die Vergangenheit akzeptieren, bevor wir die Zukunft bauen können. Deshalb stellt sich der Imperativ, das mißachtete Erbe simultan zu erforschen, untersuchen und zu interpretieren.

Die Gruppe 91 haben energisch für Dublin als eine europäische Stadt plädiert, indem sie mit ihren Gegenprojekten der 80er Jahre die Vorstellung von Dublin als einer auf das Auto ausgerichteten, 'amerikanischen' Stadt zurückwiesen. Mit ihren Vorschlägen für den 'Bachelor's Walk' lehnten sie eine umfassende Erneuerung als Verjüngungsmittel für die Innenstadt ab. Und ihre Arbeit, unter der Aegide des 'City Architecture Studio', sah die Erneuerung von Dublins Hafenvierteln Jahre, bevor die Stadtverwaltung dieses Potential erkannte, voraus. Die Gruppe 91 teilt eine Tiefe Überzeugung von städtischer Architektur und der Zukunft Dublins, die, wie sie, einem neuen Jahrtausend entgegentritt. Ihrer Arbeit liegt die These zugrunde, daß Stadtanalyse und Städtebau durch die Interaktion von verschiedenen Standpunkten, allerdings innerhalb eines allgemeinen Konsens, bereichert werden. Das ist der Grund, weshalb wir zusammen arbeiten. Wir glauben, daßß Architekten, die eine gemeinsame Grundhaltung teilen, zusammenkommen sollen, um diese Grundhaltung zu konsolidieren eine Zusammenhängende Praxis der AArchitektur von höchster Qualität zu entwickeln und Veränderungen zustande zu bringen.

Der *Bau einer modernen Sraße* versucht das traditionelle Dubliner Stadthaus neu zu interpretieren und einer Reihe neuer Stadthaustypen jene Qualitäten nahe zu bringen, die einer georgianischen Straßenreihe eigen ist und die zur Sanierung des Innenstadtgefüges angewandt werden könnten. Es ist beabsichtigt, eine Austellung von Gebäuden zu erreichen, eine moderne Wohnstraße zu bauen – die Straße neu zu errichten und das Primat des öffentlichen Bereichs wieder einzuführen. Das auserwählte Grundstück, an der Ecke zwischen Meath Street und South Earl Street auf dem 'Liberties'-Gelände ist zur Zeit baufällig. Aber 1886 baute die 'Industrial Tenements Society' auf ebendiesem Grundstück 4-geschossige Wohnhäuser, die von Charles Geoghegan entworfen worden waren – die ersten Wohnhäuser der 'philantropischen Gesellschaft' in Dublin. Nun soll das Grundstück dieses radikalen Wohnhaus-Prototyps des 19. Jahrhunderts erneut als Geburtsstätte für neue städtische Wohnhaus-Prototypen dienen, um sich unseren zeitgenössischen sozialen und ökonomischen Strukturen anzupassen. Vieles hat sich in den dazwischenliegenden Jahren verändert, und doch ist vieles gleich geblieben. Immer noch müssen wir die Lebensqualität unserer Bewohner verbessern. Unser wichtigstes Kampfmittel ist, wieder eine lebendige Stadt mit einer Mischung aller sozialen Klassen zu schaffen. Das ist die Vision, die dem Ideenprojekt *Bau einer modernen Straße* zugrundeliegt.

– Shane O'Toole

CHARTING COURSES

SOME REMARKS ON THE ARCHITECTURAL WORK OF GROUP 91

WEGMARKEN

ANMERKUNGEN ZUR ARCHITEKTUR DER 'GRUPPE 91'

There is a thread common to a number of contemporary architectural works that seek to uncover and to continue existing moments in built culture. The vividness of the visual, the visceral force of form often asserts itself as the first aspect of architectural investigation. The control of the building's appearance, the three-dimensional phenomenon absorbs much of the architect's attention. It becomes an element in the act of uncovering and linking the design of a building is called upon to enhance, strengthen or resuscitate a perceived order. It is this precise, but perhaps mute outline set by the bulk of buildings in Dublin, much of it inherited from Anglo-Saxon colonialisation, that provides an inescapable backdrop to contemporary Irish architecture.

It is interesting to study a few leaves from the portfolio of this Irish architecture so as to trace the struggle with an architectural language that gives itself, and, as a result, gives its programme and context the identical centredness or order, as did the trabeated tradition: columns, beams and walls that have found a composure in architectural configurations as well as elements of urban design. As a formal logic and as the inescapable backdrop, it is still able to resist the constant erosion by new, insensitive development. In the portfolio, we may see exceptional studies in the manner of Ludwig Mies van der Rohe and Louis Kahn, carried out by members of the preceding generation (Scott Tallon Walker, de Blacam and Meagher respectively). These studies are arguably a more direct and literal embrace of the reduced, at times abstracted post-and-lintel conceptions by Mies and Kahn, whereas the work by the younger practitioners could be said to be abstract studies of the literal logic of trabeated architecture. Some possible reasons for this could be the following. In the 1960s the 1970s, a number of architectural theorists thought the universal aspects of a built culture to have the desirable permanence from which an increasingly isolated profession would be able to draw, even though much larger-scale development was taking place against it. This stood in distinction to the outright rejection of tradition, history and context as a source for contemporary action; an attitude espoused by the ideologues of Modernism. For instance, James Stirling's references incorporated forms and the compositional syntax of the early nineteenth century architect Karl Friedrich Schinkel, broadening the former's early interest in the designs by post-revolutionary Russian architects. The supposed optimism of these so-called Constructivists was given gravitas by the renewed interest in Neo-Classicism. Within this complex

Die Absicht, bestehende Momente der Baukultur aufzudecken und fortzusetzen, zieht sich wie ein roter Faden durch eine Reihe zeitgenössischer Architekturarbeiten hindurch. Oft drängt sich die viszeral, visuelle Kraft einer Form als wichtigster Aspekt im Entwurfsprozess auf. Die Beherrschung der äußeren Erscheinung eines Gebäudes, das Phänomen der Dreidimensionalität, beansprucht zu einem Großteil die Aufmerksamkeit des Architekten. Sie wird offenbarendes und verbindendes Element zugleich, denn der architektonische Entwurf soll eine erkannte Ordnung verstärken oder wiederbeleben. Es ist diese präzise, vielleicht auch stumme Skyline von Dublin, dessen Bauten zu einem Großteil Erbe der angelsächsischen Kolonisation sind, die den unumgänglichen Hintergrund für das zeitgenössische irische Architekturgeschehen vorgeben.

Einige Seiten des Portfolios zeitgenössischer irischer Architektur genauer zu betrachten, ist deshalb von Interesse, da darin der Kampf mit einer Architektursprache aufgezeichnet ist, die sich selbst und somit ihrem eigenen Programm und Kontext dieselbe Zentriertheit oder Ordnung gibt wie die Gebälk-Architektur: Säulen, Balken und Mauern, die als Verbindungselemente in architektonischen Konfigurationen auftreten, sowie auch als städtebauliche Elemente. Diese Architektursprache bildet aufgrund ihrer formalen Logik einen Hintergrund, dem sich niemand entziehen kann, und vermag dadurch – noch – der permanenten Erosion durch eine neue, unsensible Entwicklung zu widerstehen. Wir können diesem Portfolio außergewöhnliche Studien im Geiste Ludwig Mies van der Rohes und Louis Kahns entnehmen, die von der vorhergehenden Generation ausgeführt worden waren (Scott Tallen Walker und de Blacam & Meagher). Diese Studien sind möglicherweise eine unmittelbare und wortwörtliche Vereinnahmung der reduzierten, teilweise abstrakten rationalen Konzeption von Mies und Kahn, während der jüngeren Generation als eher abstrakte Studien zur eigentlichen Logik der Gebälk-Architektur gelesen werden kann. Dafür sind folgende Erklärungen möglich: In den sechziger und siebziger Jahren glaubten einige Architekturtheoretiker, daß die universellen Aspekte der Baukultur den Anspruch der Zeitlosigkeit erfüllten, so daß sich eine zunehmende isolierte Architektenschaft darauf beziehen konnte – wenn auch die allgemeine Entwicklung in eine entgegengesetzte Richtung verlief. Damit unterschieden sie sich von den Ideologien der Moderne, die Tradition, Geschichte und Kontext als mögliche Ausgangspunkte für die

cultural mood, Leon Krier's perspectives (revisiting those by Le Corbusier) both for projects in Stirling's office as well as for his own (La Villette competition) are representative of the changed self-understanding of societies that were once again seeking assurance in a tradition, even if mythologised, of a 'timeless' order. Stirling, Krier and the Royal College of Art formed the nexus from which a number of the younger Irish architects emerged.

It would be ingenuous not to mention the continuing research that is being undertaken by students, teachers and architects into the urban and architectural history of Ireland (for instance the book by Niall McCullough and Valerie Mulvin *A Lost Tradition: The Nature of Architecture in Ireland*), research that of course is another source of influence.

The coherence of Group 91's body of work is remarkable by contemporary standards. This is evident when one surveys their last decade's oeuvre. The current design for *Making a Modern Street* is, by contrast, more differentiated than expected, and such expectations may be guided by, on the one hand, the above issues, and on the other hand the decorum normally associated with urban housing. Given all this, it is hoped that charting their courses will indicate the degrees of abstraction of the logic of trabeated architecture, with the inflection towards that which is housed or that to which the building might give an insight.

Paul Keogh's approach stands in line with those architects who have sought to provide a reticent environment constituted by conventional forms so as not to distract the users. One might argue that this is currently most successful where the design problem involves situating the design within a larger framework. The collaboration projects for Dublin City Quays (1986) gives evidence of Keogh's ability to grasp a sympathetic scale for the reconstruction of the North Quays area. Scale and building type ring true even if the specific rendition appears very close to Italian precedents (Aldo Rossi). Having finally built what exists as a suggestion only for Upper Ormond Quay (basilica and tower) in the Dairy Pavilion at Dublin Zoo (1987), Keogh's apartment building for plot 2 of the Modern Street seems to give a close account of his interest in terse and essential architecture. The design recalls more the reduced detailing of Heinrich Tessenow than the geometric, if sometimes playful purity of Rossi. Keogh's search seems to focus on that which can be said that that which needs to be said, and if it is to be said, it should find expression with the least number of elements, without

zeitgenössische Architektur vorbehaltlos ablehnten. James Stirling beispielsweise integrierte durch seine Bezugnahme auf den Architekten Karl Friedrich Schinkel dessen Formen und Kompositionssyntax in seine eigene Sprache und vertiefte dessen frühzeitiges Interesse für die russischen Architekten der Nachrevolution noch. Der angebliche Optimismus dieser sogenannten Konstruktivisten bekam eine gewisse 'gravitas' durch das neu auflebende Interesse am Neoklassizismus. In dieser komplexen kulturellen Atmosphäre verkörpern Leon Kriers Perspektiven (in Anlehnung an Le Corbusier) – die er für eigene Projekte (La-Villette-Wettbewerb) und solche von Stirling verfaßte – das veränderte Selbstverständnis einer Gesellschaft, die einmal mehr Zuflucht bei einer, wenn auch mythologisierten Tradition zeitloser Ordnung sucht. Stirling, Krier und das Royal College of Art bildeten einen Knotenpunkt, von dem zahlreiche jüngere irische Architekten ausgingen.

Es wäre ungeschickt, die kontinuierliche Forschungstätigkeit von Studenten, Professoren und Architekten zur Städtebau- und Architekturgeschichte Irlands unerwähnt zu lassen (beispielsweise das von Niall McCullough und Valerie Mulvin verfaßte Buch *Eine vergessene Tradition – das Wesen der irischen Architektur*). Diese Forschungsarbeit bildet natürlich eine zusätzliche Einflußquelle.

Die Einheitlichkeit des Gesamtwerks der 'Gruppe 91' ist, am internationalen Standard gemessen, bemerkenswert. Dies zeigt sich ganz klar, wenn man ihre Arbeit der letzten zehn Jahre überblickt. Der gegenwärtige Vorschlag für das Projekt *Bau einer modernen Straße* ist allerdings unterschiedlicher ausgefallen, als man es erwarten würde; wobei diese Erwartung möglicherweise wegen des oben genannten Sachverhalts entsteht oder aber aufgrund eines normalerweise mit städtischem Wohnbau verknüpften 'Schicklichkeitsbegriffs'. Indem hier der Weg jedes einzelnen abgesteckt wird, soll der Abstraktionsgrad ihrer Arbeit gegenüber der Logik der Gebälkarchitektur aufgezeigt werden, mit dem Hinweis auf das, was beinhaltet wird, oder auf die Erkenntnis, die der Bau vermittelt.

Paul Keoghs Ansatz entstammt dem Umfeld jener Architekten, die durch die Anwendung konventioneller Formen eine zurückhaltende Umgebung schaffen wollen, um die Benutzer nicht abzulenken. Einem solchen Vorhaben ist Erfolg beschieden, wenn bereits die Aufgabenstellung in einen größeren Rahmen gestellt wird. Das Gemeinschaftsprojekt von 1986 für die Dubliner Kais stellt Keoghs Fähigkeit unter

Paul Keogh Architects –
Pavilion at Dublin Zoo (1988)

Paul Keogh Architects –
Pavillon im Dubliner Zoo (1988)

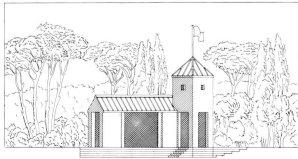

MAKING A MODERN STREET
19-20 MEATH STREET/38-41 SOUTH EARL STREET, DUBLIN 8.

subterfuge, 'invention' (as in finding a new language) or obfuscation.

Niall McCullough and Valerie Mulvin's work appears to share Keogh's premise, though, through their research as published in the above-mentioned book, the rigour of the buildings is infused by specific materials (in contradistinction to the more ubiquitous render; for instance the brickwork for the Lecture Hall for the Institution of Engineers). The diagonal line establishing the main volumes of the houses for the Modern Street is a common compositional device that is unnecessary for the clarity of the scheme. In fact, its removal might be more beneficial to the use of space in the front building. The facade development of these two houses has a maturity that suggests another aspect of the sense of order already seen in the Portico for the Abbey Theatre in Dublin.

In the work of Grafton Architects, the configuration of buildings is more sculpturally controlled, inter-twining routes with distinct volumes, as can be seen in their projects for the School at Oughterard or in the competition entry for the Táin Interpretative Centre at Carlingford. Their work refers to local and typological precedents and offers synthetic compositions, and it is possible to see devices and elements

Beweis, einfühlsam die nördliche Kai-Zone erneuern zu können. Maßstab und Bautypus scheinen richtig gewählt, auch wenn die spezifische Umsetzung sehr stark an italienische Vorbilder anzulehnen scheint Aldo Rossi). Mit dem Milchwirtschaftspavillon im Dubliner Zoo (1987) realisierte er schließlich, was nur andeutungsweise beim Upper-Ormond-Kai in Erscheinung tritt (Basilika und Turm). Mit seinem Wohnbau auf Grundstück 2 für das Ideenprojekt *Bau einer modernen Straße* scheint er klare Rechenschaft über sein Interesse an knapper und reduzierter Architektur abzulegen. Dieses Projekt erinnert eher an Heinrich Tessenows knappe Detailbehandlung als an die geometrische, wenn auch manchmal spielerische Klarheit Rossis. Keogh konzentriert sich in seiner Suche eher auf das, was gesagt werden kann, als auf das, was gesagt werden muß; und wenn es gesagt werden muß, soll es sich durch die kleinstmögliche Anzahl von Elementen ausdrücken, ohne Ausflüchte, Erfindungen (wie etwa das Entdecken einer neuen Sprache) oder Verschleierungen.

Niall McCullough und Valerie Mulvin scheinen Keoghs Grundsätze zu teilen, obwohl die Strenge ihrer Bauten – aufgrund ihrer Forschungstätigkeit für das bereits erwähnte Buch – durch die Verwendung spezifischer Materialien geprägt ist. Das Backsteinmauerwerk der Vorlesungshalle für den Ingenieur-Verband beispielsweise hebt sich deutlich von den allgegenwärtigen Verputzfassaden Dublins ab. Mit der diagonalen Ausrichtung der Hauptvolumen ihrer Häuser für den *Bau einer modernen Straße* greifen sie auf ein geläufiges Kompositionsmittel zurück, das allerdings nicht zur Deutlichkeit der Lösung beiträgt. Tatsächlich wäre es der Raumnutzung der Vorderseite sogar förderlich, wenn sie darauf verzichteten. Die Fassadengestaltung dieser beiden Häuser izeigt eine Reife, die einen Aspekt ihres Ordnungssinnes andeutet, den sie bereits beim Portikus für das Abbey-Theater in Dublin unter Beweis stellten.

Bei den Arbeiten der Grafton Architects zeigt sich, daß die Anordnung der Bauten aufgrund ihrer skulpturalen Eigenschaften bestimmt wird. Gehwege werden mit den verschiedenen Volumen verflochten, wie das auch beim Schulhausbau von Oughterard oder bei ihrem Wettbewerbsbeitrag für das Táin-Interpretative-Centre in Carlingford ersichtlich ist. Ihre Architektur bezieht sich auf regionale und typologische Beispiele und weist synthetische Kompositionen auf; aber auch von Stirlings Erweiterungsbau der Stuttgarter Staatsgalerie übernommene Elemente und Grundsätze sind ablesbar. Der verdichtende Bau am Ormond-Kai zeugt von einer Bewußtheit und Entschiedenheit, wie sie

McCullough Mulvin Architects – Institution of Engineers Lecture Hall (1989)

McCullough Mulvin Architects – Vorlesungshalle für den Ingenieur-Verband (1989)

Grafton Architects – Secondary School at Oughterard, Co Galway (1991)

Grafton Architects – Schulhaus in Oughterard, County Galway (1991)

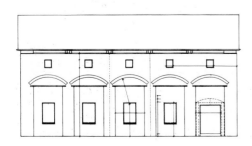

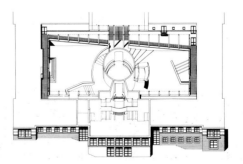

from Stirling's addition to the Stuttgart Staatsgalerie. The infill building on Ormond Quay displays an awareness and resolution that is rare for such difficult contexts. It is nevertheless telling to see the new superstructure align itself more closely to its neighbouring bank building than the neo-gothic base on which it stands. Another possibility might have been to build something that, while deferring to its surroundings, makes something independent. The proposal for the Modern Street could become such a relatively independent piece, a quality that significantly extends to the physical relation between the residents, irrespective of the centering courtyard.

Michael McGarry and Siobhan NíEanaigh have demonstrated a fine sense of construction, detailing and formal control. The Brick House is at once an abstraction of rural buildings while at the same time engaging in the discussion of the visual richness of seemingly haphazard aggregated volumes. Its almost didactic constructional details suggest a concern for the revaluation of the meaning of trabeation. Partial symmetries, oppositions, pairings and couplings give evidence of a dense set of intentions that have been realised in a sober way.

The Municipal Theatre in Galway, designed by Derek Tynan and the Urban Design Unit, NBA, appears to respond to many urban pressures, to the extent that the composition retains an additive character rather than professing a whole; the recourse to applied configural elements (curving bay windows, etc) does not resolve the ambivalence between a fragmentary composition and an urban collage. In the design for a double house for Belgrave Square in Monkstown, Derek Tynan develops the linear house with adjacent corridor element, seen earlier on in the Carberry House. The later version allows the corridor to read as an independent volume, taking on the role as a connecting element between the new and the old. Rooms and building configurations in these latter schemes are subject to greater and more assured control than in the case of the Theatre.

The meeting ground between McGarry NíEanaigh and Derek Tynan is the single family house type in the countryside; the House on a Drumlin and Carbery House at Ardreigh Lock respectively. Their joint proposal for the Modern Street is convincing in some instances, the basic massing, the dual aspect towards the streets, the piano nobile from which the grand stairway to the units rises. While the Irish climate is relatively mild, the openness and grandeur of the stairway do

selten in einem solch schwierigen Kontext erreicht werden können. Allerdings verrät er auch gerade selbst, daß sein Oberbau stärker auf das angrenzende Bankgebäude als auf die neo-gothische Basis bezogen ist, auf der er steht. Eine andere Möglichkeit hätte darin bestanden, durch Verweis auf die Umgebung die eigene Unabhängigkeit zu verdeutlichen. Mit ihrem Vorschlag für den *Bau einer modernen Straße* erreichen sie eine solche, relative Unabhängigkeit, was auch für die physische, vom zentralen Innenhof unbeeinflußte Beziehung zwischen den Bewohnern zutrifft.

Michael McGarry und Siobhan NíEanaigh besitzen einen subtilen Sinn für Konstruktion, Detailbehandlung und Form. Beim 'Brick'-Haus handelt es sich einerseits um eine Abstraktion von ländlichen Bauten, anderseits thematisiert es die visuelle Reichhaltigkeit scheinbar zufällig miteinander verbundener Volumen. Die beinahe didaktisch wirkenden Konstruktionsdetails verweisen auf eine neuwertende Auseinandersetzung über die Bedeutung der Gebälkarchitektur. Teilsymmetrien, Gegenüberstellungen, Paarungen und Kopplungen zeugen von einer konzentrierten Absicht, die auf eine nüchterne Art verwirklicht wurde.

Das Stadttheater von Galway, von Derek Tynan an der Abteilung für Städtebau des NBA (National Building Agency) entworfen, scheint sich auf viele städtebauliche Kräfte zu beziehen, in dem Sinne, daß die Komposition einen antithetischen Charakter beibehält anstatt eine Ganzheit zu wollen; der Rekurs auf applizierte Baukörperelemente (geschwungener Erker usw.) löst die Ambivalenz zwischen fragmentarischer Komposition und städtebaulicher Collage nicht. Im Entwurf für das Doppelhaus am Belgrave Square entwickelt Derek Tynan, wie schon beim Carbery-Haus, einen länglichen Baukörper mit einem seitlichen Korridor. Der Korridor, der die Funktion eines Verbindungsteils zwischen alt und neu übernimmt, wird so zu einem unabhängigen Volumen. Im Vergleich zum Stadttheater von Galway weisen die späteren Entwürfe eine grössere Sicherheit in Bezug auf die räumliche und formale Gestaltung auf.

McGarry / NíEanaighs und Derek Tynans Projekte für ländliche Bauten – 'Bauernhaus auf einem Hügel' beziehungsweise das Carbery-Haus in Ardreigh Lock – weisen Gemeinsamkeiten auf. Ihr in Partnerschaft ausgearbeiteter Vorschlag für den *Bau einer modernen Straße* überzeugt hinsichtlich Volumetrie, der Doppelgesichtigkeit des Eckbaus und durch das Piano-Nobile, von dem aus das Treppenhaus zu den oberen Einheiten führt. Obschon das irische Klima

McGarry NíÉanaigh Architects – Brick House facing the Mourne Mountains (1990)

McGarry NíÉanaigh Architects – Backstein-Wohnhaus gegen die Mourne Mountains (1990)

Derek Tynan Architects – Carberry House at Athy, Co Kildare (1988)

Derek Tynan Architects – Carberry-Einfamilienhaus in Athy, County Kildare (1988)

not seem to make the best possible use of resources: space and energy. The covered area in front of the stairs at pavement level would be confusing. Having said this, with such an achievement as the Brick House, there would be no doubt that this corner apartment unit could be as good as that.

In Shay Cleary's relatively long list of completed buildings, it is possible to discern a further source of influence for members of Group 91: the Maison de Verre (or Maison Delsace) in Paris. The wider references are the afore-mentioned Russian Constructivists. Cleary has combined them in his work with his penchant for emphasising serial configurations. Thus we see the 'subdivision' of configurations that one would otherwise expect to be more unitary (Houses at Swan Place and Raglan Road, Dublin). We see this again as if it were a signature in the street facade to his houses for the Modern Street. Perhaps the motif is a homage to Le Corbusier's Atelier for Amedée Ozenfant in Paris of the 1920s. The space between the two houses is almost entirely occupied by a winding staircase. Its presence is overbearing for both the space as well as for those apartments overlooking the court, and its relocation would prompt either the introduction of plants or the re-dimensioning of the space. His ability to arrive at a successful resolution is undoubted as his work to the Royal Hospital Kilmainham shows. The building has been adapted to house paintings in three wings, with sculptures shown in the courtyard. The portico, marking the main entrance and sitting within the courtyard, is a succinct addition, fittingly representing the shared ideal of the members of Group 91: trabeated architecture, neutral, well-proportioned elements in dialogue with the immediate context.

Sheila O'Donnell and John Tuomey have spent a long time on the Irish Film Centre. This project is now going ahead. It brings together the exchange between historical substance and new programmes: the new auditorium is located within the enclosure of an old church. An indirect path leads through the site. One of the entrances is marked by a new corner building, whose configuration and windows relate both to the neighbouring building as well as indicating the public quality of the space in between. The sense of order revealed here is not as yet present in their house for the Modern Street. The street facade's subdivision, the numerous openings of different proportions, the mixture of brickwork and the steel trussed 'bracket' do not have the same sense of mastery as the Irish Pavilion for Leeuwarden reconstructed in the

relativ mild ist, scheinen Ressourcen Raum und Energie aufgrund der Offenheit und Großmaßstäblichkeit des Treppenhauses nicht optimal genutzt. Der vor dem Treppenhaus auf Erdgeschoßebene angelegte und überdachte Platz verwirrt eher. Zieht man die beim 'Brick'-Haus vollbrachte Leistung in Betracht, so besteht allerdings kein Zweifel darüber, daß auch dieses Eckwohnhaus qualitativ nicht nachstehen müßte.

Shay Clearys langer Liste realisierter Gebäude läßt sich eine weitere Einflußquelle der Gruppe 91 entnehmen: Die 'Maison de Verre' oder 'Maison Dalsace' in Paris, und, von noch größerer Bedeutung, die russischen Konstruktivisten. Cleary kombiniert diese Einflüsse mit seiner Vorliebe für betonte serielle Anordnungen. Dadurch erklärt sich die 'Unterteilung' von Konfigurationen, von denen man sich sonst eine größere Einheitlichkeit versprochen hätte (Häuser am Swan Place und an der Raglan Road in Dublin). Wie ein kennzeichnendes Merkmal erkennen wir dieses Motiv an der Straßenfassade seines Projektes für den Bau einer modernen Straße wieder. Vielleicht ist es als Hommage an das von Le Corbusier in den zwanziger Jahren gebaute Atelier für Amédéé Ozenfant in Paris gedacht. Eine Wendeltreppe füllt den Raum zwischen den beiden Häusern fast ganz aus. Sie ist sowohl für diesen Zwischenraum als auch für die hofseitigen Wohnungen von zu wuchtiger Präsenz, doch eine Versetzung würde entweder eine Redimensionierung des Platzes oder eine Bepflanzung erfordern. Seine Fähigkeit, erfolgreiche Lösungen zu finden, ist aber unbestritten, wie sein Vorschlag für das Royal Hospital Kilmainham beweist. Es wurde umgebaut, um eine Gemäldesammlung in drei Hausflügeln unterbringen und Skulpturen im Garten ausstellen zu können. Der in den Garten gestellte Portikus kennzeichnet den Haupteingang. Er stellt eine kurzgefaßte, knappe Erweiterung dar und steht damit für das gemeinsame Ideal der Gruppe 91: Gebälkarchitektur, neutrale, gut proportionierte Elemente im Dialog mit dem unmittelbaren Kontext.

Sheila O'Donnell und John Tuomey arbeiteten lange am Projekt des irischen Filmzentrums, das jetzt realisiert wird. Es bringt historische Substanz in den Dialog mit neuen Programmen: das neue Auditorium steht nämlich innerhalb der Einfriedungsmauer einer alten Kirche. Ein indirekter Weg führt durch das Grundstück. Einer der Eingänge wird durch ein neues Eckgebäude gekennzeichnet, das durch seine Konfiguration und Anordnung der Fenster auf das Nachbargebäude, aber auch den Öffentlichkeitscharakter des Zwischenraums verweist. Der hier zum Ausdruck kommende

Shay Cleary Architects –
Houses at Raglan Road, Dublin
(1989)

Shay Cleary Architects –
Wohnhäuser an der Raglan
Road, Dublin (1989)

O'Donnell and Tuomey Architects
Irish Film Centre, Temple Bar
(construction 1991)

O'Donnell and Tuomey Architects
Irisches Filmzentrum, Temple-
Bar (realisation 1991)

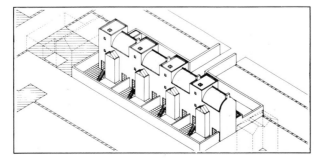

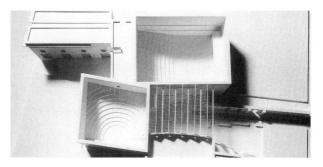

courtyard of the Royal Hospital Kilmainham. With this building, O'Donnell and Tuomey's work appears to have moved away from the close adherence to trabeated buildings to the pursuit of the evocative aspect of sculptural form. This is another direction of figuration, one in which the programme (in the case of the Pavilion, the work of the painter) gives a strong impetus to the definition of a building's mass. In the pavilion, there is a dense and complex relation between configuration and contents.

The poetry of the minimal, the love of ruins, of fragments set within a rugged landscape are aspects to which Shane O'Toole's work aspires. In his proposal for the Modern Street it is therefore not surprising to see two 'Ivory Towers' on top of the main bodies of the houses. At street level there is a discreet skin, silent and planar; set back and idealised as cubes there the individual's 'penthouses', aloof and remote from daily activities. His studies of the mausoleum and the Fountain Wall of the Fourteen Tribes indicate an interest in reduction, essence, essential forms. Detailing and materials are not subservient to the idea, in fact, O'Toole's work embraces the complexity that these aspects bring: his primary aim appears to be the most succinct representation of the basic idea.

We have charted a few courses. We have mapped out some similarities and some differences. As a group, these architects share common premises. As a group, they will have a profound effect on Irish architecture. They are keeping their minds open, so as to develop their work by engaging in frank discussions. This exhibition is an invitation to join these discussions and to expand that common premise.

– Wilfried Wang, May 1991

Sinn für Ordnungen ist in ihrem Beitrag zum *Bau einer modernen Straße* weniger ausgeprägt. Die Gliederung der Straßenfassade, die verschieden proportionierten Öffnungen sowie die Mischung aus Backsteinmauern und Eisenbetonträgern weisen nicht denselben Grad an Meisterschaft auf wie der im Innenhof des Royal Hospital wiederaufgebaute Irische Pavillon einer in den Niederlanden gezeigten Ausstellung. Mit diesem Bau scheinen sich O'Donnell und Tuomey von den Grundsätzen der Gebälkarchitektur zu entfernen und dem evokativen Aspekt einer skulpturalen Form nachzuspüren. Damit begeben sie sich in eine neue Richtung der Formgebung, indem die Aufgabenstellung eines Projekts – im Falle des Pavillons das Werk eines Malers – einen starken Antrieb bei der Definierung der Baumasse bildet. Beim Pavillon äußert sich eine enge und komplexe Beziehung zwischen Konfiguration und Inhalt.

Die Poesie des Minimalen, die Liebe für Ruinen und für in einer rauhen Landschaft plazierte Fragmente sind Aspekte, die Shane O'Toole in seiner Arbeit anstrebt. Es erstaunt deshalb nicht weiter, daß er in seinem Vorschlag für den *Bau einer modernen Straße* zwei 'Elfenbeintürme' auf die Hauptkörper der Bauten aufsetzt. Auf Straßenebene hat er eine diskrete, ruhige und ebene Haut angebracht; die Penthäuser für Einzelpersonen sind zurückversetzt und als Kuben idealisiert, abseits und weit weg von den Alltagsaktivitäten. Seine Studien zum 'Mausoleum' und zur 'Mauer mit Springbrunnen für die vierzehn Stämme' zeugen von seinem Interesse für Reduzierung auf das Wesentliche, für reduzierte Formen. Detailbehandlung und Materialwahl stehen der Idee nicht nach. Tatsächlich beinhaltet O'Tooles Werk die Komplexität, die diese Aspekte mit sich bringen: In erster Linie scheint er eine äußerst knappe Umsetzung seiner Grundidee anzustreben.

Wir haben einige Wege, etliche Gemeinsamkeiten und einige Unterschiede aufgezeichnet. Als eine Gruppe teilen diese Architekten gemeinsame Grundsätze. Als eine Gruppe werden sie die irische Architektur stark beeinflussen. Um ihre Arbeit weiterentwickeln zu können, wollen sie ihre Offenheit behalten und die Diskussion weiterführen. Diese Ausstellung ist als Einladung zur Diskussion gedacht, mit der Absicht, das gemeinsame Ideengut bereichern zu können.

– Wilfried Wang, Mai 1991

O'Donnell and Tuomey Architects Irish Pavilion – 11 Cities/11 Nations (Neths '90, Dublin '91)

O'Donnell and Tuomey Architects Irischer Pavillon – 11 Städte/11 Nationen (Nied. '90, Dublin '91)

Shane O'Toole Architect – Von Rohr Mausoleum, Newstown, Co Carlow (1986)

Shane O'Toole Architect – Von Rohr Mausoleum, Newstown (Carlow) 1986

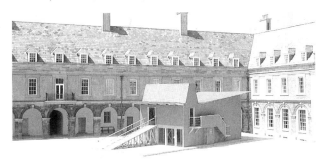

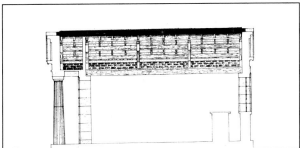

INTRODUCTION

EINLEITUNG

These proposals are a continuation of over ten years' work on a diverse range of urban design projects. This work in the past has taken the form of competition entries, publications and exhibitions, including one of the same title which formed part of the Independent Artists' Exhibition of 1980 and which was initiated by our friend and colleague, the late Michael de Courcy.

The intention of this project is to build a modern residential street, a built exhibition, offering a range of new urban house types which could inform the reconstruction of our four- and five-storey residential streets. It is our conviction that the rebuilding of Dublin needs to take place at the scale of small infill sites, in addition to the larger scale redevelopment of derelict areas in the city.

These seven plots are equal in area, but vary in frontage and in depth, and relate in scale to the typical Georgian plot, the grain of the city. The scheme includes shops, workshops and offices, together with a whole range of apartment designs and sizes – 31 apartments in all. The architecture illustrates a wish to overlay on our tradition a delight and an excitement about modern architecture, maximising space, light, transparency and movement within the density of urban building.

Intended for construction, the project has been designed within the commercial constraints of typical urban apartment developments, and planning permission has been obtained for all but one of the buildings, where the interests of other parties have yet to be resolved. The project has been a collaborative venture involving architects, project managers, quantity surveyors, engineers, lawyers, valuers and graphic designers. The project is sited on the corner of Meath Street and South Earl Street in the Liberties. The site is owned by Dublin Corporation and has been offered to Group 91 as a contribution to Dublin 1991 – European City of Culture.

– *Shelley McNamara*

Diese Vorschläge setzen eine über zehnjährige Arbeit an städtebaulichen Projekten fort. Diese erfolgte in Form von Wettbewerbsbeiträgen, Publikationen und Ausstellungen, darunter auch die gleichnamige im Rahmen der Ausstellung unabhängiger Künstler im Jahre 1980, die von unserem verstorbenen Freund und Kollegen Michael de Courcy angeregt wurde.

Das von ihm ins Leben gerufene Projekt bezweckt den Bau einer modernen Straße mit Wohnhäusern, die als gebaute Ausstellung realisiert werden sollte. Es stellt eine Reihe neuer Stadtwohnhaus-Typen zur Auswahl und dient als Modell für die Erneuerung der 4- und 5-geschossigen Straßenbebauungen Dublins. Wir sind davon überzeugt, daß die Erneuerung Dublins einerseits durch Verdichtung, anderseits durch umfassende Sanierung baufälliger Zonen innerhalb der Stadt erfolgen muß.

Die sieben Grundstücke des Projektes sind gleich groß, variieren allerdings bezüglich Breite und Tiefe. Sie beziehen sich auf das klassische georgianische Grundstück, die kleinste Zelle der Stadt. Im Programm vorgesehen sind der Bau von Läden, Werkstätten und Büroräumen, nebst 31 Wohnungen verschiedenster Größe und Beschaffenheit. Die Architektur dieser Bauten illustriert unseren Wunsch, von der Tradition ausgehend, unserer Freude und Begeisterung an moderner Architektur Ausdruck zu geben, die es ermöglicht, Raum, Licht, Transparenz und Bewegung in einem Gebäude zu optimieren.

Das zur Realisierung vorgesehene Projekt ist unter Berücksichtigung der ökonomischen Sachzwänge, die sich städtebaulichen Projekten stellen, geplant worden. Die Baubewilligung wurde für alle Bauten außer einem – wo die Interessensgegensätze noch gelöst werden müssen – erteilt. Das Projekt war ein Gemeinschaftsunternehmen von Architekten, Bauherren, Ingenieuren und Juristen. Dieses Eckgrundstück zwischen Meath Street und South Earl Street liegt auf dem 'Liberties'-Gelände. Eigentümer ist die 'Dublin Corporation', die es der Gruppe 91 als Beitrag im Rahmen von 'Dublin 1991 – Europäische Kulturstadt' zur Verfügung stellte.

– *Shelley McNamara*

photo: Peter Barrow

Group 91 Project Team

Project Managers	New Ireland Project Managers Ltd
Group 91 Architects	Shay Cleary Architects
	Grafton Architects
	Paul Keogh Architects
	McCullough Mulvin Architects
	McGarry NíÉanaigh Architects
	O'Donnell and Tuomey Architects
	Shane O'Toole Architect
	Derek Tynan Architects
Consulting Engineers	Brian Hendrick & Associates
Quantity Surveyors	Austin Reddy & Company
Valuers & Estate Agents	Sherry Fitzgerald Ltd
Solicitors	Eugene F Collins & Son

Folgende Beraterteams und Architekturbüros waren am Projekt beteiligt:

Projektleitung	New Ireland Project Managers Ltd
Architekten der Gruppe 91	Shay Cleary Architects
	Grafton Architects
	Paul Keogh Architects
	McCullough Mulvin Architects
	McGarry NíÉanaigh Architects
	O'Donnell Tuomey Architects
	Shane O'Toole Architect
	Derek Tynan Architects
Ingenieursbüro	Brian Hendrick & Associates
Bauspezialisten	Austin Reddy & Company
	Sherry Fitzgerald Ltd
Juristen	Eugene F Collins & Son

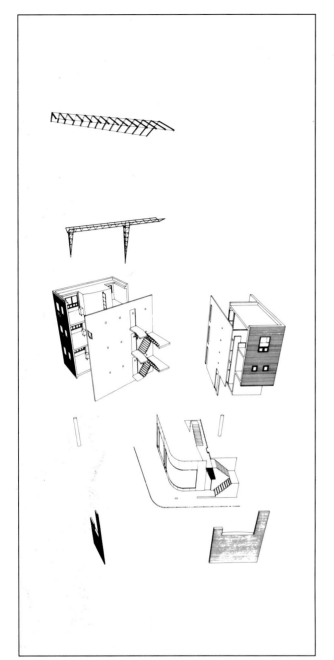

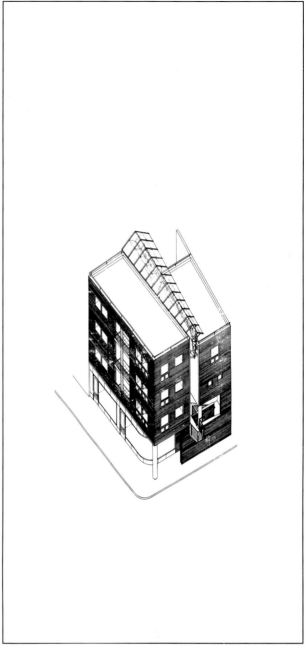

**Plot 1: McGarry NíÉanaigh Architects /
Derek Tynan Architects**

This proposal is for the corner site at the junction of Meath Street with South Earl Street. The design is concerned with the expression of that particular corner position and a generalised proposition about the design of mixed use urban buildings, necessary to maintain and foster the vitality of the city.

The proposal has retail use on the ground floor, fronting onto Meath Street, coincident with the existing scale and character of the street. The shops form a base above which are two almost independent buildings sharing an upper level courtyard. This courtyard is entered from a gated stairway on Earl Street and forms an open but canopied space shared by the apartments. There are two apartment types – a three-storey 'house' onto South Earl Street and three single-level apartments onto Meath Street.

The street facades will be brick, with metal shopfronts, windows and balconies. The internal elevation of the courtyard will be rendered and painted, as are the corner columns on Meath Street. The courtyard canopy will be steel and glass.

**Grundstück 1: McGarry NíÉanaigh Architects /
Derek Tynan Architects**

Dieser Bebauungsvorschlag für das Eckgrundstück zwischen Meath Street und South Earl Street weist zwei Frontseiten auf. Mit dem Entwurf soll die besondere Ecksituation zum Ausdruck gebracht, aber auch ein allgemeingültiger Vorschlag für Überbauungen mit Mischnutzungen präsentiert werden, um so die Vitalität der Stadt aufrechterhalten und fördern zu können.

Gegen die Meath Street wird das Erdgeschoß, dem Maßstab und Charakter der Straße entsprechend, für Geschäfte genutzt. Sie bilden eine Basis, auf die zwei nahezu unabhängige Bauvolumen aufgesetzt sind, die einen gemeinsamen Hof im Obergeschoß teilen. Dieser Hof ist von der Earl Street durch ein Tor über eine Treppe zugänglich und bildet einen offenen, aber überdachten Raum, mit Zugang zu den Wohnungen. Es gibt zwei Wohnungstypen: ein dreigeschossiges 'Haus' gegen die South Earl Street und drei eingeschossige Wohnungen gegen die Meath Street.

Die Straßen-Fassaden aus Backstein-Mauerwerk weisen Ladenfronten, Fensterrahmen und Balkone aus Metall auf. Der Innenhof soll gestaltet und bemalt werden so wie die Ecksäulen gegen die Meath Street. Für die Überdachung des Innenhofs ist eine Glas-Stahl-Konstruktion vorgesehen.

GROUND FLOOR   FIRST FLOOR   SECOND FLOOR   THIRD FLOOR   CROSS SECTION

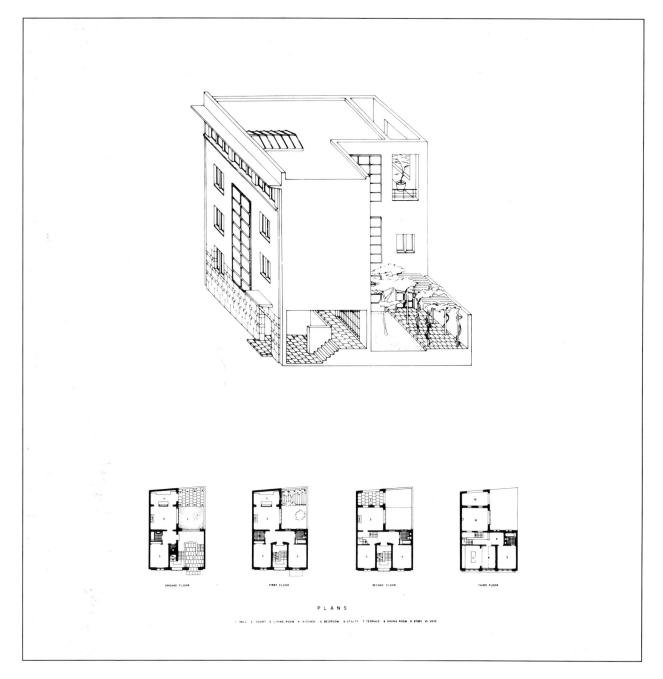

PLANS

1 HALL 2 COURT 3 LIVING ROOM 4 KITCHEN 5 BEDROOM 6 UTILITY 7 TERRACE 8 DINING ROOM 9 STUDY 10 VOID

GROUND FLOOR   FIRST FLOOR   SECOND FLOOR   THIRD FLOOR

Plot 2: Paul Keogh Architects

The building contains three apartments of various sizes, grouped around an enclosed south-facing courtyard which is available to all the residents of the building.

The street entrance opens into a generous hallway leading onto the courtyard and from which the main staircase accesses the upper-floor apartments. The ground floor contains a one-bedroom apartment with its own private terrace and pergola. The first floor contains a two-bedroom apartment while the upper floors consist of a larger two-bedroom apartment which has its own private terrace with views of the Dublin mountains.

The design of the larger apartments is based on the small 19th century Dublin artisan's house. The sectional organisation comprises a grand living room to which bedrooms and kitchens are subservient. The main living rooms are located in the return and have large west-facing studio windows to take advantage of the views and orientation. The apartments are flexible in their layout and the generosity of the spatial arrangement of these apartments is designed to offer an exciting alternative to people who want to live in an urban situation.

The elevational treatment of the building is clearly defined in brick with a stone base, a large stairhall surrounded by the bedroom windows on either side.

Grundstück 2: Paul Keogh Architects

Die drei unterschiedlich großen Wohnungen dieses Wohnhauses umschließen einen nach Süden gerichteten Hof, der allen Bewohnern des Gebäudes zugänglich ist.

Von der Straße her tritt man in eine großzügige Eingangshalle, die zum Innenhof führt, von dem aus das Treppenhaus, zu den oberen Geschossen führt. Das Erdgeschoß enthält eine 2-Zimmerwohnung, mit eigener Terrasse und Pergola. Im ersten Stock ist eine 3-Zimmerwohnung, im 3 und 4 Stock ist eine größere 3 Zimmerwohnung geplant. die eine Dachterrasse mit Ausblick auf die Dubliner Berge hat.

Die größeren Wohnungen nehmen auf die für Dublin typischen Handwerkerhäuschen aus dem 19 Jahrhundert Bezug. Die Unterteilung beinhaltet einen sehr großen Wohnraum, dem Schlafzimmer und Küche untergeordnet sind. Die Hauptwohnräume befinden sich im Seitenflügel und haben große atelierartige Fenster gegen Westen, die die Aussicht voll nützen, die die Lage des Grundstückes bietet. Die Wohnungen weisen einen flexiblen Grundriß auf.

Die Fassaden sind durch das Backstein Mauerwerk über einer Naturstein-Basis klar definiert. Die hohe Fensterfront des Treppenhauses ist links und rechts von kleineren Schlafzimmerfenstern umrahmt.

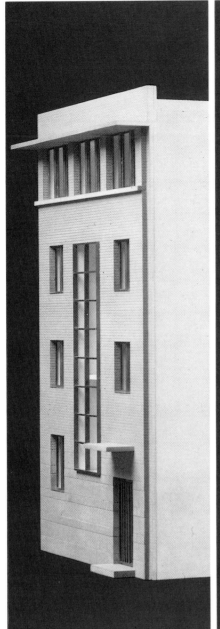

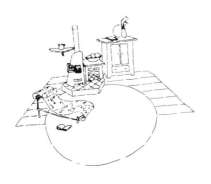

Plot 3: O'Donnell & Tuomey Architects

This scheme is designed like a large house with varying floor to ceiling heights in proportion to room-sizes and providing a wide range of apartment types and sizes. It comprises 1 office, 1 car space, 1 studio, 1 one-bed, 1 two-bed and one three-bed apartment with each unit designed to be distinctive and take advantage of different locations within the building. The street elevation is intended to indicate and display the variety of accommodation in the building. Apartments are accessed from the glass-roofed common stair. The apartments have high ceilinged living rooms with double aspect overlooking the street and providing views to the south to the Dublin mountains.

Grundstück 3: O'Donnell & Tuomey Achitects

Dieses Büro-Wohnhaus wurde nach dem Vorbild eines 'großen Hauses' mit verschiedenen, zur Fläche proportionalen Raumhöhen entworfen. Es besitzt verschiedene Wohnungstypen, von unterschiedlicher Größe: je eine 2-, 3-, und 4-Zimmerwohnung sowie ein Büro, eine Garage und ein Atelier. Die verschiedenen Einheiten heben sich klar voneinander abund sind so entworfen, daß sie ihre verschiedenen Lagen innerhalb des Gebäudes voll nützen. Ihre Unterschiedlichkeit soll schon aus der Straßenfassade ablesbar sein. Die Wohnungen sind über eine gemeinsame, glasüberdachte Treppe erschlossen. Die hohen Wohnzimmer bieten einen Ausblick auf die Straße und die Dubliner Berge im Süden.

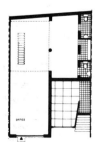

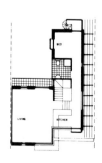

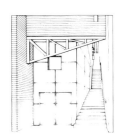

Plot 4: Grafton Architects

On our 6 metre frontage site we chose to examine a modern interpretation of the typical Dublin house type with its front block to the street and 'mews' behind.

The building is entered through an archway, which allows access for cars, and maintains an openness at ground level, with glimpses from the street to the inner world of the building. The full depth of the plot is accentuated by the placement of the stairs and terrace to the mews behind on axis with this entrance. This 'break' in the back wall allows south light to penetrate deep into the site and is also the eye of the scheme, with views to the Dublin mountains in the distance.

All circulation is open and leads directly from the archway and from the courtyard.

In the composition of the front elevation the first floor balcony and the ground floor archway are combined to make a large doorway to the inner court.

Grundstück 4: Grafton Architects

Auf diesem nur 6 Meter breiten Grundstück wollten wir die moderne Interpretation eines für Dublin typischen Wohnhauses` – ein Straßenblock mit Hinterhaus – wagen und prüfen.

Durch einen Torbogen, der auch Autos Zufahrt gewährt, wird das Gebäude betreten. Diese Transparenz der Erdgeschoßebene erlaubt Einblicke in das 'Innenleben' des Hauses. Die Grundstückstiefe wird durch die in der Fluchtlinie des Eingangs liegenden Treppe und Terrasse der Hinterhäuser noch betont. Eine große Öffnung in der Rückfassade des Hinterhauses läßt das Sonnenlicht in das Grundstück eindringen und erlaubt den Ausblick auf die Dubliner Berge in der Ferne.

Alle Wohnungen sind vom Durchgang und von der Innenhofseite her erschlossen. Für die Fassadengestaltung wurde der Balkon im ersten Obergeschoß mit dem Torbogen kombiniert. So erscheint der Durchgang zum Innenhof optisch größer.

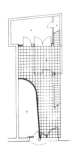

GROUND FLOOR   FIRST FLOOR   SECOND FLOOR   THIRD FLOOR   FOURTH FLOOR   ROOF PLAN

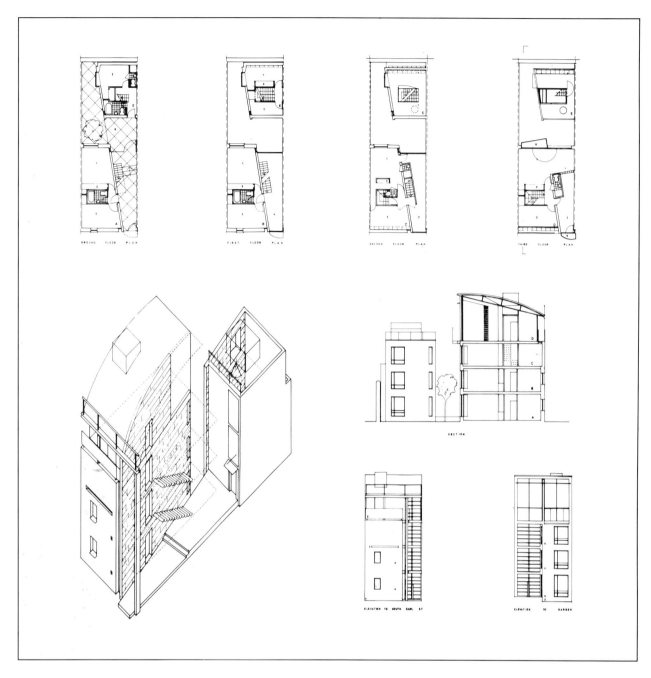

Plot 5: McCullough Mulvin Architects

The long narrow site suggested a re-interpretation of the classic Dublin plot, traditionally occupied by house and mews. It is based on the same hierarchy – a larger 'house' to the street and a smaller tower/mews in the garden.

The proposal takes advantage of the depth of the site: the large window in the front elevation directs a view to the facade of the tower – in effect, the building is a frontal composition with two elevations, where the eye is drawn in and light from the rere filters onto Earl Street.

The site plan is organised to support this, with a large spine wall in coloured plaster sloping across the plot. This wall defines two zones of space, each anchored by a solid service and circulation block. The wall becomes a penetrating element cutting a series of parallel planes and organising the main space of the building.

The facade to the street has been developed with an asymmetric balance between the brick panel, the glazed screen and the wall which punctures it. Secondary elements – the sheet-steel balcony, windows and steel channels play a secondary game across it in a lighter rhythm.

Grundstück 5: McCullough Mulvin Architects

Das tiefe und schmale Grundstück suggerierte eine Neuinterpretation des klassischen Dubliner Wohnhauses mit Hinterhaus. Das Projekt beruht auf derselben Hierarchie – mit einem großen Hauptgebäude gegen die Straße und einem kleineren Hinterhaus im Garten. Die Tiefe des Grundstücks wird zu seinem Vorteil genutzt: Das große Fenster in der Straßenfassade erlaubt einen Durchblick auf das Hinterhaus, hier als Turmhaus konzipiert. Das Projekt ist eine Komposition zweier vertikaler Flächen, deren Transparenz das Auge ins Innere lockt und es der Südsonne erlaubt, bis zur Earl Street durchzudringen.

Der Grundriß des Entwurfs betont dies mit einer großen farbig verputzten Mauer, die wie ein Rückgrat schräg durch das Grundstuuck verläuft. Diese Mauer definiert zwei keilförmige Zonen, die glauben lassen, daß das Hinterhaus aus dem Hauptgebäude herauswächst und formt so eine Beziehung zwischen den beiden. Die Mauer wird so ein durchdringendes Element, das eine Reihe paralleler Ebenen schneidet und den Zwischenraum der Gebäude organisiert.

Die Straßenfassade zeigt ein assymetrisches Gleichgewicht zwischen der geschlossen wirkenden Backsteinwand und dem vollständig verglasten Wandschlitz mit dem integrierten Durchgangstor. Elemente wie Metallbalken, -fenster und andere Metallprofile sind von zweitrangiger Bedeutung.

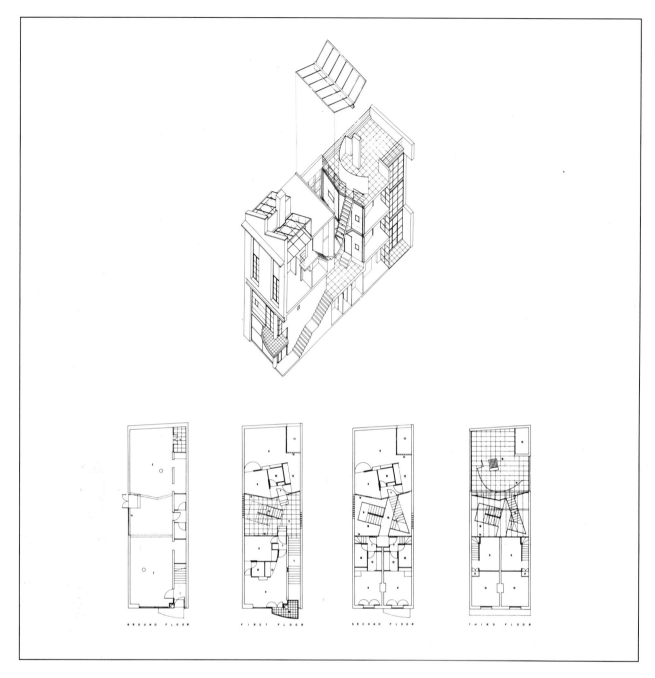

GROUND FLOOR   FIRST FLOOR   SECOND FLOOR   THIRD FLOOR

Plot 6: Shay Cleary Architects

The scheme is for a narrow-frontage urban infill site. It comprises a ground floor of office/commercial with five one-bedroom apartments above. The project was taken as an opportunity to experiment with small-scale, high-density urban living units and their aggregation.

The apartments are accessed via a straight-flight cascading staircase which leads to first-floor level. A lightwell penetrates the scheme and contains an eccentric steel staircase. This stairs leads to a bridge at second floor and onto a shared south-facing roof terrace above and would become an important social element in the scheme where chance meetings and conversation could take place. Three of the apartments are horizontal in arrangement and two are duplexes. They are all between 350-400 sq. ft. in area. In spite of their small square footage they will have a certain spatial generosity by being either open-plan or volumetrically arranged depending on unit type. The common roof terrace and access stair assume an intended importance and use because of the small dwelling size.

The street facade is of brick, with steel, glass and concrete insertions. The elevations to the lightwell are of glass block. A steel and glass rooflight shelters the common stair. Windows and screen would be steel.

Grundstück 6: Shay Cleary Architects

Der Entwurf bezieht sich auf eine schmale, vorder- und hinterfrontbezogene Grundstücklücke. Er bietet im Erdgeschoß Nutzungen für Läden und Büros, in den Obergeschossen fünf 2-Zimmerwohnungen. Mit diesem Projekt wurde die Gelegenheit erriffen, mit kleinmaßstäblichen, verdichtenden Wohneinheiten zu experimentieren. Die Wohnungen sind über eine gerade, steile Treppe, die direkt ins 1. Obergeschoß führt, erschlossen. Ein Lichthof, in dem eine exzentrisch geführte Stahltreppe verläuft, durchdringt das Volumen. Diese Treppe führt ins 2. Obergeschoß auf eine Verbindungsbrücke, von der aus eine weitere Treppe zu der gemeinsamen, nach Süden orientierten Dachterrasse hinaufführt. Diese Terrasse wird ein wichtiges soziales Element des Entwurfs, da sie zufällige Begegnungen und Gespräche ermöglicht. Drei Wohnungen sind als Etagenwohnungen angelegt, und zwei sind Maisonette-Wohnungen. Sie sind alle ca 35 qm groß. Trotz ihrer kleinen Grundfläche besitzen sie aufgrund eines offenen Grundrisses oder der volumetrischen Anordnung eine gewisse räumliche Großzügigkeit. Die gemeinsame Dachterrasse und Verbindungstreppe erfüllen wegen der geringen Wohnungsgrößen eine wichtige Funktion. Die Straßenfassade besteht aus Backstein-Mauerwerk, das von Stahl Glas- und Betonelementen durchbrochen ist. Die Seitenfassaden des Lichthofes sind aus Glasziegeln gefertigt. Ein Glas-Stahloberlicht schützt die gemeinsame Treppe. Die Öffnungssysteme sind aus Metall konstruiert.

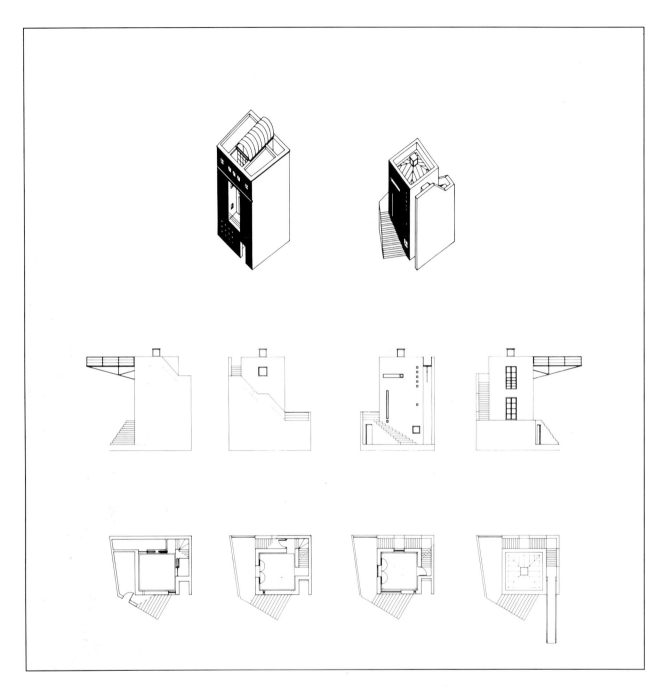

Plot 7: Shane O'Toole Architect

The different character of each of these three houses responds to its location on the site. The 'street house', lit through a glass-block drum, is remarkable for its two-storey balcony onto the street and is, perhaps, rather solemn in its expression. The 'tower house' is enigmatic, holding secret the mysteries of its internalised world. The barrel-vaulted 'sky house', perched above the street house and reached by a precarious bridge from a cascading staircase which spirals around the tower house, has a distant focus – the rooftops and spires of the city, the mountains to the south. In my mind's eye, I can see Jacques Tati, 'Mon Oncle', descending by a most convoluted route from his rooftop shack – now disappearing from view, now reappearing behind some opening in the wall. By the time he has reached the street, he has established for us the community of neighbours.

Design Team: Shane O'Toole with Antoinette O'Neill.

Grundstück 7: Shane O'Toole Architect

Die verschiedenen Charaktere dieser drei Häuser sind eine Antwort auf ihre unterschiedliche Lage auf dem Grundstück. Das 'Straßenhaus', durch einen transparenten Dombau aus Glasziegeln erhellt, ist durch einen zweigeschossigen Balkon zur Straße hin geprägt und hat einen eher würdevollen Ausdruck. Das rätselhafte 'Turmhaus' behält die Geheimnisse seiner verinnerlichten Welt für sich. Das 'Wolkenhaus' mit dem Tonnendach, das auf dem, 'Straßenhaus' aufsitzt und über einen Gefahr andeutenden Steg von einer steilen Treppe, die sich um das Turmhaus windet, zugänglich ist, überblickt die Hausdächer und Türme der Stadt und die im Süden gelegenen Berge. Vor meinem inneren Auge sehe ich Jacques Tati – 'Mon Oncle' – den gewundenen Weg von seiner Dachhütte hinuntersteigen, bald hinter einer Mauer verschwindend, bald hinter einer Öffnung wiederauftauchend. Hat er die Straße erreicht, so hat er für uns die Gemeinschaft der Nachbarn etabliert.

Verfasser: Shane O'Toole mit Antoinette O'Neill.

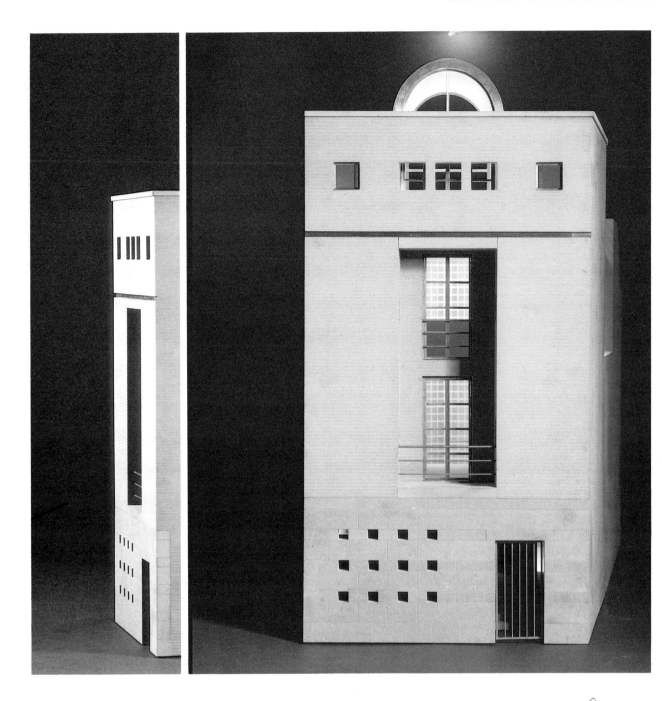

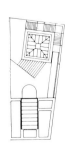

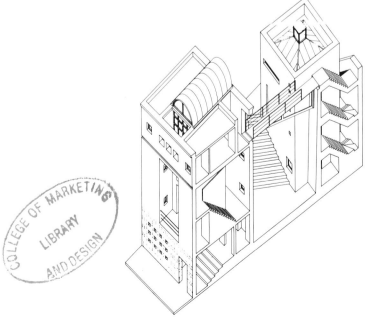

1 – McGARRY NíÉANAIGH ARCHITECTS and DEREK TYNAN ARCHITECTS / 2 – PAUL KEOGH ARCHITECTS / 3 – O'DONNELL AND TUOMEY ARCHITECTS

/ 4 – GRAFTON ARCHITECTS / 5 – McCULLOUGH MULVIN ARCHITECTS / 6 – SHAY CLEARY ARCHITECTS / 7 – SHANE O'TOOLE ARCHITECT

SHAY CLEARY
ARCHITECTS

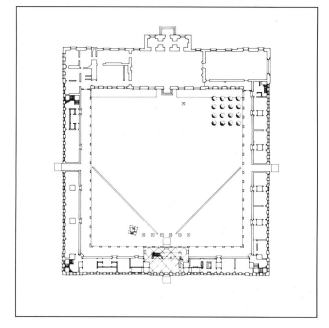

Graduated from School of Architecture, University College Dublin. in 1974. Commenced private practice in 1977 having worked in Paris and London for Marcel Breuer and Candilis Josic and Woods. Has built urban housing and apartments and has been involved more recently in public commissions. Has exhibited and lectured widely and has been published in Ireland and Europe. Was a visiting critic to Princeton University Graduate School in 1989. Received the AAI Downes Medal for work to the Point Depot in 1989. Currently architect for the Irish Museum of Modern Art at the Royal Hospital Kilmainham.

———

Er promovierte 1974 an der Architekturfakultät des University College in Dublin. Nachdem er in Paris und London für Marcel Breuer und Candilis Josic & Woods gearbeitet hatte, eröffnete er 1977 sein eigenes Architekturbüro. Nebst Projekten für Stadtwohnhäuser und -wohnungen ist er seit kurzem auch mit öffentlichen Projekten beauftragt worden. Er nahm an einer Reihe von Ausstellungen und Vorträgen teil, und seine Arbeiten wurden in Irland und Europa publiziert. 1989 war er Gastkritiker an der 'Princeton University Graduate School'. Für das 'Point Depot'-Projekt erhielt er 1989 die 'AAI Downes Medal'. Er wurde kürzlich vom Irischen Museum für Moderne Kunst mit dem Umbau des Royal Hospital Kilmainham beauftragt.

Collaborators and assistants / Mitarbeiter und Assistenten – John Dorman, Sam Gaine, Frank Hall (Partner 1980-86), Brian McClean, Alan Mee, David Naessens, Esmonde O'Briain, Eilis O'Donnell, Dominic Stevens, Derek Tynan

Irish Museum of Modern Art, Royal Hospital Kilmainham (1990)

The project involves the conversion of three sides of this seventeenth century building to house the new Museum of Modern Art. The scheme proposes the making of a new entrance hall axially related to the existing Great Hall. This new Hall will volumetrically connect the entrance to the first floor (where the main permanent collection is housed) by means of a steel and glass staircase in a double-height volume. The repetitive rooms are being retained as far as possible with minor alterations to gain more wall space. The existing courtyard will have a new rolled fine-gravel surface with stone pathways and will become the largest room of the museum for sculpture and external installations. All new elements in the scheme are consciously modern and minimal to contrast with the historic stone building.

Umbau des Royal Hospital Kilmainham für das Irische Museum für Moderne Kunst (1990)

Das Projekt sieht den Umbau von drei Flügeln dieses Gebäudes aus dem 17. Jahrhundert vor, damit sie vom Irischen Museum für Moderne Kunst neu genutzt werden können. Geplant ist der Anbau einer neuen Eingangshalle, die auf der Achse der großen Halle liegen soll. In diesem Neubau stellt eine aus Stahl und Glas gefertigte, doppelgeschossige Treppe die volumetrische Verbindung zwischen dem Eingang und dem 1. Obergeschoß her, wo der Großteil der ständigen Sammlung untergebracht werden soll. Die repetitive Anordnung der Räume soll so weit wie möglich beibehalten werden – es sind nur geringfügige, Platz schaffende Änderungen vorgesehen. Der bestehende Hofraum, der als größter Ausstellungsraum für Skulpturen und Installationen im Freien genutzt werden soll, wird mit einer feinen Kiesschicht bedeckt und durch gepflasterte Gehwege erschlossen. Die absichtlich modern und minimal gestalteten neuen Elemente kontrastieren mit der historischen Bausubstanz.

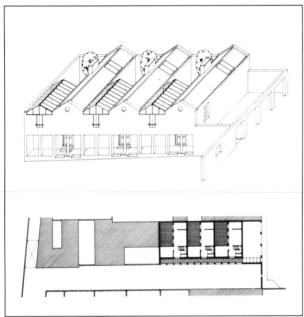

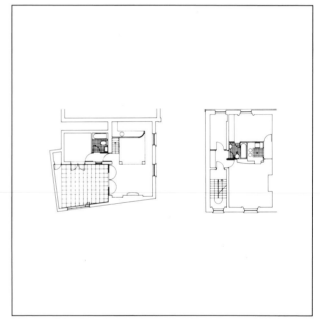

Houses at Swan Place (1983) *left*

The scheme consists of three town-houses on a narrow mews lane. A house type was proposed consisting of two parallel bays both 3.3m wide and their gables expressed on the street. The longer bay had entrance hall, staircase, master bedroom and bathroom at ground floor and living and kitchen at upper level. The shorter bay had a second bedroom/study at ground floor with a dining room in a conservatory above. The outdoor space or 'room' is contained by two-storey walls and is addressed by the main rooms of the house.

Apartments Harcourt Terrace (1984) *right*

The existing pair of Regency houses were in a totally dilapidated condition. A completely new interior structure was placed within the historic envelope. A variety of apartments was created ranging from the conversion of the Annexe into a painters studio, to smaller one and two bedroom units in the main houses. All of the units in their design optimise the use of rooflighting or double-height spaces.

Wohnhäuser am Swan-Platz (1983) *links*

Das Projekt besteht aus drei an einer schmalen Gasse liegenden Reihenhäusern. Jedes Haus besteht aus zwei längsgerichteten, 3,3 Meter breiten Gebäudekörpern mit eigenen Giebeldächern. Im längeren sind im Erdgeschoß Eingangshalle, Treppenhaus, Eltern-Schlafzimmer und Badezimmer untergebracht, im oberen Geschoß Wohnzimmer und Küche. Im Erdgeschoß des kürzeren Gebäudekörpers befinden sich ein zweites Arbeits-/Schlafzimmer und im Obergeschoß ein Wintergarten als Eßzimmer. Die wichtigsten Zimmer haben einen Ausblick auf den Innenhof, der durch eine hohe, bis ins Obergeschoß reichende Mauer begrenzt wird.

Renovation zweier Wohnhäuser an der Harcourt Terrace (1984) *rechts*

Die beiden im Regentenstil gebauten Wohnhäuser befanden sich in einem sehr baufälligen Zustand. Eine vollkommen neue Struktur wurde in die historische Gebäudehülle eingefügt. Verschiedene Wohnungstypen wurden geschaffen. Das Nebengebäude wurde in ein Malatelier umgebaut, während die Hauptgebäude 2- bis 4-Zimmerwohnungen enthalten. Alle Wohneinheiten sind durch die Anwendung von Oberlichtern und doppelgeschossigen Räumen optimiert.

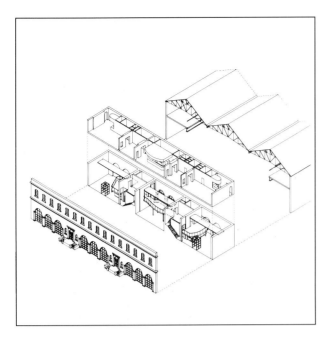

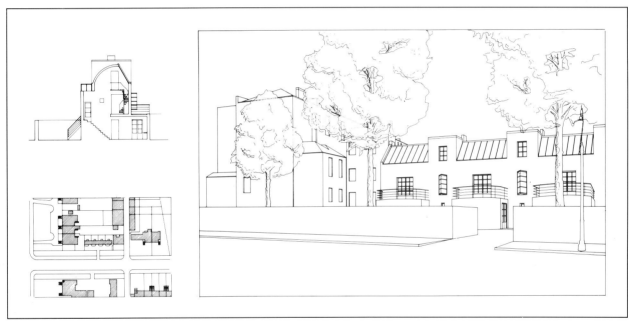

Entrance Hall, Bar and Restaurant, Point Depot National Exhibition Centre (1990)

The Point Depot was built in 1878 as a goods warehouse for the Great Southern and Western Railways and consists of a cast-iron 'shed' with a formal front to the river in the form of a masonry building 8m deep and 50m long. The scheme for the bar consists of two end-spaces and a gallery level which joins them. This gallery level connects the three spaces axially and becomes a bridge as it passes through the entrance hall. The services and lighting in each stone space are carried on a suspended service platform which acts as another element axially connecting the three major spaces. All new interventions are consciously precise and polychromatic to contrast with the stone envelope.

Houses at Raglan Road (1989)

The site in question was originally the back garden of an eighteenth century town house. It has a long frontage to the secondary road. The scheme proposes a three-storey house type which is extremely narrow in section because of the shallow site. It has very little aspect to the rear to avoid overlooking. Living is at first-floor level with a vaulted curved ceiling. Various elements project from the main terrace form and give the houses an added complexity and dimension.

Eingangshalle, Bar und Restaurant im 'Point Depot National Exhibition Centre' (1990)

Das 'Point Depot', ein Warenlagerhaus, Baujahr 1878, umfaßt eine Gesamtfläche. Es besteht aus einer gußeisernen Halle und einem 8m tiefen und 50m langen, dieser Halle vorgelagerten Gebäude in Massivbau, das die Vorderfront gegen die Flußseite bildet. Die beiden Bars, die sich in den zwei Gebäudeenden der Seitenflügel befinden, sind durch eine die Eingangshalle durchquerende Galerie verbunden. Gebäudeausrüstung und Beleuchtung sind in einer aufgehängten Plattform untergebracht, die ein weiteres axiales Verbindungselement der drei Hauptvolumen darstellt. Die Eingriffe sind durch Präzision und einen farbigen Reflexanstrich gekennzeichnet, um sie deutlich von der Gebäudehülle aus Naturstein abzuheben.

Wohnhäuser an der Raglan Road (1989)

Das Grundstück war früher der Hintergarten eines Stadthauses aus dem 18. Jahrhundert. Die geplanten dreistöckigen Häuser haben aufgrund der beschränkten Grundstückstiefe einen außergewöhnlich schmalen Querschnitt. Die Rückfassade wird nur durch wenige, kleine Fensteröffnungen unterbrochen, um ihre Privatsphäre zu bewahren. Das Wohnzimmer im Erdgeschoß wird von einer gewölbten Decke begrenzt. Die vorspringenden Raumelemente geben dem Bau eine zusätzliche Komplexität und Dimension.

GRAFTON ARCHITECTS

The partners of Grafton Architects, Yvonne Farrell, Shelley McNamara and Tony Murphy, graduated from the School of Architecture, UCD in 1974. Having worked in Dublin, Paris and London, they established Grafton Architects in 1977. Their work includes private houses, apartments, schools and urban infill. Teaching in UCD since 1976; visiting critics to AA and RCA, London in 1981; University of Jordan, 1982. Lectured on their work in RIBA, London and RIAI, Cork, 1990. The School in Oughterard, was one of two Irish projects chosen for 'Architecture Publique 1990' at the Pompidou Centre, Paris.

——

Yvonne Farrell, Shelley McNamara und Tony Murphy promovierten 1974 an der Architekturfakultät des UCD. Bevor sie 1977 ihr eigenes Architekturbüro eröffneten, sammelten sie in Dublin, Paris und London erste Praxiserfahrung. Ihr Werk umfaßt Privathäuser, Wohnungen, Schulen und Vedichtungsbau. Seit 1976 unterrichten sie an der Architekturfakultät des UCD. Sie waren Gastkritiker an der AA und am RCA in London im Jahr 1981 sowie an der University of Jordan im Jahr 1982. 1990 hielten sie einen Vortrag über ihr Werk am RIBA in London und am RIAI in Cork. Das sich im Bau befindliche Schulhaus in Oughterard (Galway) war eines der beiden ausgewählten irischen Projekte, die an der Ausstellung von öffentlichen Bauten 1990 im Centre Pompidou in Paris gezeigt wurden.

——

Assistants – Esmonde O'Briain, Tracy Staunton, Eoin St John Downes

Apartments, Pembroke Road, Dublin (1986)

The top floor of a four-storey Victorian house is converted into two apartments. The volume and structure of the existing roof is revealed; new dynamic elements are inserted – diagonal staircase, double height volumes with large rooflights, roof terrace and balcony.

House at Ticknock, Co Dublin (1977)

Built for his parents, Tony Murphy based this house on Le Corbusier's petite villa on the shore of Lake Geneva.

——

Umbau eines Dachgeschosses an der Pembroke Road, Dublin (1986)

Das Dachgeschoß eines 4-geschossigen viktorianischen Hauses wurde zu zwei Wohnungen ausgebaut. Volumen und Struktur des Daches wurden freigelegt und mit neuen dynamischen Elementen ergänzt: eine diagonal angelegte Treppe, zweigeschossige Volumen mit großen Oberlichtern, eine Dachterrasse und ein Balkon.

Einfamilienhaus in Ticknock, Dublin (1977)

Mit diesem Einfamilienhaus für seine Eltern nahm Tony Murphy auf Le Corbusiers 'Petite villa' am Genferseeufer Bezug.

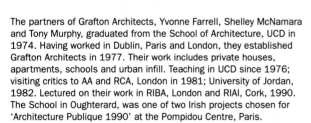

Infill Building at Ormond Quay, Dublin (1989)

Situated on the quays of the river Liffey, facing south, this infill building stands on the site of a Presbyterian Church, the ruins of which still remained. The ornate neo-gothic limestone base was retained for its memory and its quality. This gives the building a presence and stature, other than the small scale domestic and absorbs and integrates these architectural remnants, adding to the rich collage of time and elements, that is the nature of City. This building was completed in 1989.

Füllen einer Baulücke am Ormond-Kai in Dublin (1989)

Dieses am Ufer des Liffey-Flußes gelegene Gebäude wurde über einer Ruine einer alten presbyterianischen Kirche errichtet. Die reichverzierte neo-gotische Kalksteinbasis, die aufgrund ihres guten Zustandes zur Erinnerung bewahrt wurde, verleiht dem Gebäude eine sich klar von den Nachbarbauten unterscheidende Gestalt, absorbiert und integriert diese architektonischen Reste und trägt damit zur reichen Collage der Zeit und Elemente bei, die das Wesen der Stadt ausmachen. Das doppelgeschossige Fenster mit den freistehenden Säulen in der Fassadenmitte soll als neues und modernes Element gelesen werden. Das Gebäude wurde 1989 fertiggestellt.

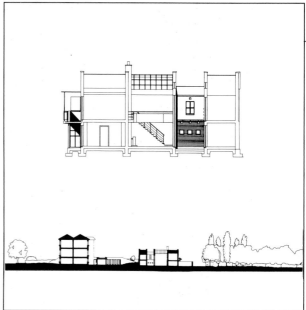

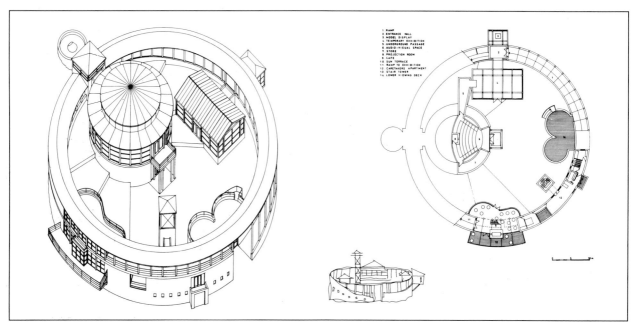

Studio (1983) and Mews (1989), Clyde Lane, Dublin

These two mews complete the development of a Victorian plot between Clyde Road and Clyde Lane. Clyde Lane is unique in Dublin, as it is a mews lane which faces south and enjoys a view out over Herbert Park. In 1978, the main Victorian house was renovated; then a sunken grass-roofed garden Studio was added; now the plot is to be completed by two mews.

Each mews is designed around a series of courtyards, facing the sun and the view. The whole organisation can be described as a living 'house' to the front/sun/park and a sleeping 'house' to the rear. The design takes as its inspiration the traditional mews, which refers to either workshops or stables in the expression and rejects totally the new suburban-type mews, which ignores the existence of this context.

The Tain Interpretative Centre at Carlingford, Co Louth (1988)

The Tain saga is the Celtic equivalent of the Iliad. This project is based on the interpretation of Iron Age ring fort settlements, still evident in the Irish landscape. The scheme makes a thick enclosing wall, acting as a container for the objects within. The building itself was seen as an exhibit, which would evoke the atmosphere of the past and not just a container of historic objects. This was a competition entry in 1988.

Reihenhäuschen mit Atelier an der Clyde Lane, Dublin (1983/89)

Diese beiden Reihenhäuschen vervollständigen die Erneuerung eines viktorianischen Grundstücks zwischen Clyde Road und Clyde Lane. Dieser Straßenzug mit Hinterhäusern ist insofern einzigartig für Dublin, als daß er nach Süden, gegen den Herbert-Park ausgerichtet ist. 1978 wurde das viktorianische Hauptgebäude renoviert, später wurde ein versenktes grasüberwachsenes Atelier hinzugefügt, und nun wird es noch um diese zwei Reihenhäuschen erweitert. Beide Häuschen sind um mehrere Innenhöfe herum, zur Sonne und gegen den Park hin, angelegt. Die Wohnräume sind auf der Straßenseite, die Schlafräume auf der Hofseite untergebracht. Der Entwurf bezieht sich auf das traditionelle Hinterhaus, das einst als Werkstätte oder Stall genutzt wurde, und lehnt damit den neuen Reihenhaustypus der Vorstädte ab, die einen solchen wertvollen Kontext ignorieren.

Das Tain-Kulturinstitut in Carlingford (Louth) 1988

Der Tain-Epos ist das keltische Gegenstück der Illiade. Dieser Wettbewerbsbeitrag stellt eine Neuinterpretation der kreisförmigen Festungsbebauungen aus der Eisenzeit dar, die heute noch vereinzelt in der irischen Landschaft zu sehen sind. Eine dicke Festungsmauer fungiert als Behälter für die eingeschlossenen Baukörper. Das Hauptgebäude ist selbst als Ausstellungsstück gedacht, das die Vergangenheit heraufbeschwören soll.

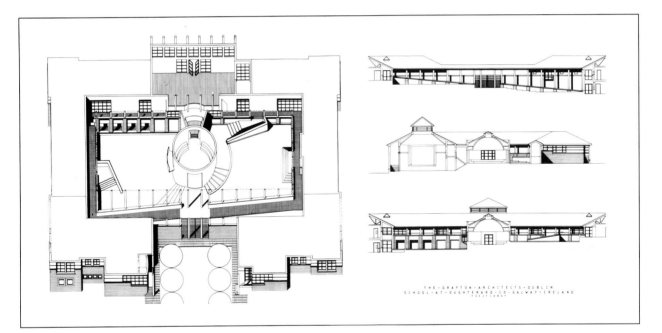

THE·GRAFTON·ARCHITECTS·DUBLIN
SCHOOL·AT·OUGHTERARD·CO·GALWAY·IRELAND
·SECTIONS·

School Extension, Lisdoonvarna, Co Clare (1983) *top*

This scheme makes a courtyard, with a new entrance, between the old and the new school. The new classroom block is connected to the existing by means of the double-height volume of the gymnasium. Thos space is thought about as an extension of the court, and has a gallery connection at first floor level.

Secondary School at Oughterard, Co Galway (1991) *bottom*

This school building for 350 pupils is located in the outskirts of the picturesque village of Oughterard in the west of Ireland. The site slopes from northwest to south east and is exposed to strong prevailing winds. The scheme proposes an enclosed courtyard, which offers protection from the winds and creates a micro-climate, allowing students to circulate in this space with pleasure and in comfort.

The plan of the school is based on the monastic plan. The Assembly Hall sits as an object in the main courtyard, as does the 'lavabo' in the cloister of the 12th century Cistercian Monastery, at Mellifont. This building is under construction.

Schulhaus in Lisdoonvarna (Clare) 1983 *oben*

Dieser Plan schafft einen Hof mit neuem Eingang zwischen der alten und der neuen Schule. Der neue Klassenblock ist mit dem vorhandenen durch die doppelt sohohe Turnhalle verbunden. Dieser Raum ist als Erweiterung des Hofs gedacht und hat in der Höhe des ersten Stocks eine Galerie Verbindung.

Schulhaus in Oughterard (Galway) 1991 *unten*

Dieses Schulhaus für 350 Schüler liegt am Rande des malerischen Dorfes Oughterard in Westirland. Das Gelände fällt von Nordwesten nach Südosten ab und ist starkem Wind ausgesetzt. Der Entwurf sieht einen geschlossenen Innenhof vor, der Schutz vor dem Wind gewährt und ein Mikroklima schafft, was es den Schülern erlaubt, sich ungestört darin aufhalten zu können.

Die Anlage bezieht sich auf den Grundriß eines Klosters. Die Versammlungshalle liegt wie ein Objekt im Innenhof, wie das auch schon beim 'Lavabo' des Zisterzienserklosters von Mellinfont aus dem 12. Jahrhundert der Fall war. Das Schulhaus befindet sich gegenwärtig im Bau.

PAUL KEOGH ARCHITECTS

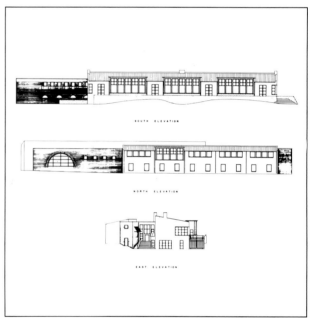

Established in 1984, the work of Paul Keogh Architects has been published and exhibited in Ireland and abroad and has won numerous awards, including an AAI award in 1989 and first prize in the Goldsmiths Company jewellery shop competition. The principals of the practice are Paul Keogh and Rachael Chidlow.

Paul Keogh studied at UCD and at the Royal College of Art in London. He has worked for James Stirling, Michael Wilford and Associates, de Blacam and Meagher and the OPW. Rachael Chidlow studied interior design at Manchester Polytechnic and Environmental Design at the RCA. She worked with de Blacam and Meagher.

——

Das Architekturbüro Paul Keogh Architects besteht seit 1984. Ihre Arbeiten sind in Irland selbst, aber auch im Ausland veröffentlicht und ausgestellt worden. Sie wurden mehrfach ausgezeichnet, u.a. mit dem AAI-Preis im Jahr 1989 und dem ersten Preis im Wettbewerb der Goldsmith Company für den Entwurf eines Bijouterie-Geschäfts. Chefarchitekten sind Paul Keogh und Rachael Chidlow.

Paul Keogh studierte am UCD und am Royal College of Art in London. Er arbeitete im Architekturbüro von James Stirling, Michael Wilford & Associates, bei de Blacam & Meagher und für das städtische Hochbauamt. Rachael Chidlow studierte Innenarchitektur am Polytechnikum von Manchester und 'Environmental Design' am RCA. War sie im Büro von de Blacam & Meagher angestellt.

Assistants / Assistenten – Cathy Curran, Helena Fitzgerald, John MacPolin, Frank McGahon, John McLaughlin, Billy Nolan, David Power

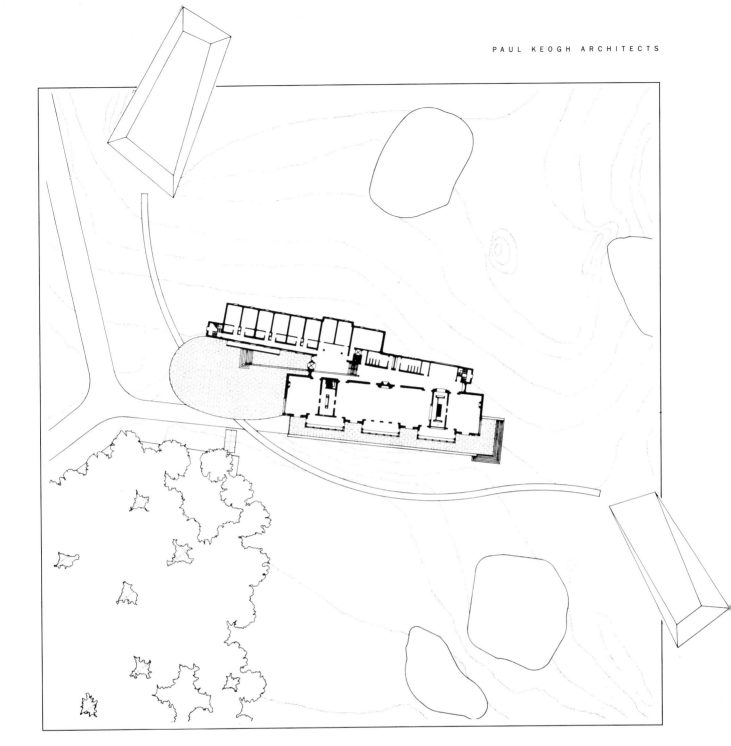

Golf and Country Club Hotel, Delgany, Co Wicklow (1990-)

This project is located in Co Wicklow, approximately 20 miles south of Dublin. The site is bounded by the sea to the east and the views to the north are dominated by the Sugar Loaf Mountain and Bray Head in the distance.

The building contains three large public rooms which are located so as to have southern views over the golf course: a restaurant, reception room and bar, each of which have large conservatories with views over the golf course and in particular the 18th green.

The hotel wing forms a wall to the entrance court and the bedrooms, located on the eastern side of this entrance court are orientated towards the sea. The changing facilities and service accommodation are located beneath the public rooms, thus elevating the main social areas to above the surrounding landscape. The layering of the plan is used to reduce the scale of the building and to create a strong identity for each functional component of the building.

Golf- und Country-Clubhotel in Delganey (Wicklow) 1990-

Dieses Hotelprojekt liegt im County Wickow, ungefähr 20 Meilen südlich von Dublin. Das Grundstück stößt im Osten ans Meer. Die Aussicht im Norden wird durch den Sugar Loaf Mountain und den Bray Head beherrscht.

Die drei großen Hallen im Haupttrakt mit Empfang, Restaurant und Bar sind je einem Wintergarten angeschlossen, von wo aus der Golfplatz überblickt werden kann, besonders das 18.Grün. Der Trakt mit den gegen das Meer gerichteten Hotelzimmern bildet eine Mauer im Eingangshof. Garderoben und Dienstleistungen liegen im unteren Stock, so daß die drei Hallen wo sich das soziale Leben abspielt, über der Landschaft liegen.

Die Grundriß-Schichten sollen den Maßstab der Überbauung raffen, um die Identität der einzelnen Funktionsbereiche deutlich zu kennzeichnen.

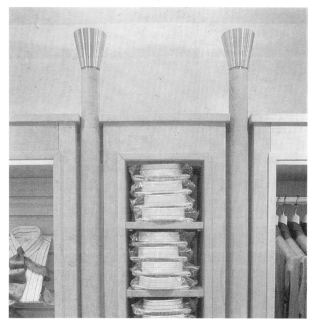 

Pavilion at Dublin Zoo (1988)

The Zoo Pavilion is a milking parlour for a single cow in Dublin Zoo, set within a small amphitheatre built to demonstrate the milking process to children. The tower forms a place from which the milk is served to children. The materials and composition of the building were made to evoke the idea of simple traditional farmyard buildings.

Cabinet detail for Diffney's Manshop, Blackrock, Co Dublin (1985)

The interior is lined with oak and individual cabinets made to display menswear.

Garden Room at Percy Place, Dublin (1989)

This project consists of the addition of sin gle room to an existing 1940s end-of-terrace house at Percy Place, Dublin. A single-pitched structure, its gable to the canal and, in order to take advantage of orientation, it is glazed on its south and west elevation. Internally the room is vaulted to counteract its open aspect and give focus to the dining table.

Pavillon im Dubliner Zoo (1988)

Der Pavillon im Dubliner Zoo ist ein Melkraum für eine einzige kuh, in ein kleines Amphitheater gebaut, um Kindern das Melken anschaulich vorzuführen. Der Turm bildet den Platz, von dem die Zusammensetzung des Gebäudes sollen an einfache traditionelle Bauernhof Gebäude erinnern.

Schauschränkedetails für Diffney's Manshop, Blackrock, Co Dublin (1985)

Der Inneraum ist mit Eiche verkleidet und verschiedene Schränke wurden gebaut, um Herrenkleidung zur Schau zu stellen.

Gartenzimmer am Percy Place, Dublin (1989)

Dieses Projekt istder Anbau eines einzigen Zimmers an ein End-Reihenhaus aus den 40-er Jahren am Percy Place, Dublin. Eine Struktur mit Giebel zum Kanal und um diese Lage voll zu nützen ist ihre Süd und Westseite verglast. Innen ist der Raum gewölbt im Gegensatz zu seiner Offenheit und konzentriert sich so auf den Eßtisch.

LIVING ROOM - WEST TERRACE

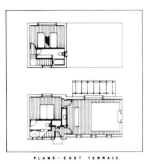

PLANS - EAST TERRACE

PATIO - EAST TERRACE

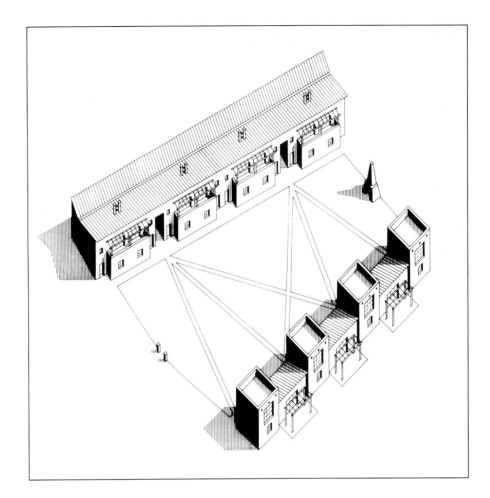

Holiday Houses at Velvet Strand Portmarnock (1990-)

This project consists of a proposal for sixteen holiday houses at Velvet Strand, Portmarnock, Co Dublin.

It is proposed to retain the existing stable buildings and walled paddocks within the design for the project and to develop twelve new houses surrounding a landscaped garden on the eastern portion of the site.

The new houses are in two terraces surrounding a garden in the tradition of collegiate plans and almshouses. They are arranged to take advantage of the panorama over the golf course and of Howth Head to the south. They also orientate themselves towards the sea: the continuous terrace on the west boundary having views of the dunes through the towers of the east terrace towards the sea.

The garden, containing a communal barbecue area, overlooks the golf course to the south. It is grassed and has informal tree planting in the manner of a common. It is crossed by narrow paths connecting the entrance yard to the tower houses.

Ferienhäuser am Velvet-Strand in Portmarnock (1990-)

Der Entwurf beinhaltet einen Vorschlag für 16 Ferienhäuser am Velvet-Strand in Portmarnock, County Dublin.

Die bestehenden Ställe und umzäunten Koppeln sollen in das Projekt integriert und 12 Neubauten um eine gestaltete Gartenanlage im östlichen Grundstücksteil herum angelegt werden.

Die Neubauten bestehen aus zwei Häuserzeilen, die in der Tradition britischer Colleges und Altersheime einen Garten umschließen. Ihre Anordnung erlaubt eine optimale Panoramasicht auf denGolfplatz und Howth Head im Süden. Die Zeilen selber sind zum Meer hingerichtet: die westliche Häuserzeile gewinnt zwischen den Türmen der östlichen Häuserzeile hindurch Aussicht auf die Dünen.

Der Garten, der mit einer gemeinschaftlichen Grillanlage ausgestattet ist läßt den Blick auf den Golfplatz im Süden offen. Er ist mit Rasen bedeckt und mit Bäumen in spielerischer Anordnung bepflanzt,wie ein öffentlicher Park. Schmale Gehwege verbinden den Eingangshof mit den Turmhäusern.

McCULLOUGH MULVIN
ARCHITECTS

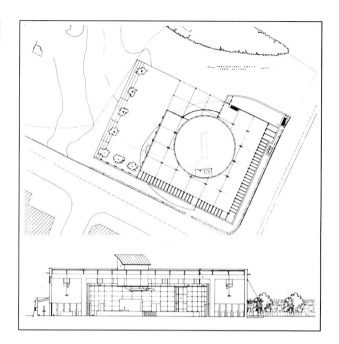

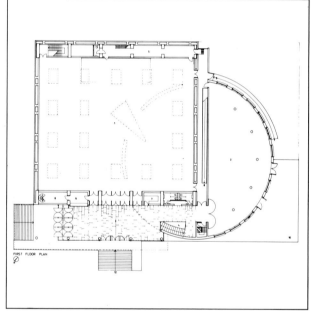

Graduated School of Architecture, UCD. in 1981, and spent a post-graduate year in Rome. Commenced private practice in 1985 and are tutors in School of Architecture, Bolton Street, Dublin. Have exhibited and lectured widely in Europe and America. Have published two books: 'A Lost Tradition – The Nature of Architecture in Ireland' (1987) and 'Dublin – An Urban History' (1989). Their built work includes the Abbey Theatre Portico, Dublin; Conversion of the Free Church, North Charles Street, Dublin (Ford Conservation Award 1990); and Lecture Hall, Dublin, for the Institution of Engineers (Architectural Association of Ireland Award 1989).

———

Beide promovierten im Jahr 1981 an der Architekturfakultät des University College in Dublin und machten Nachdiplomstudien in Rom. Sie eröffneten 1985 ein eigenes Architekturbüro. Heute sind sie als Tutoren an der Architekturfakultät in Dublin tätig. Sie nahmen an zahlreichen Ausstellungen und Vorträgen in Europa und Amerika teil. Sie publizierten zwei Bücher:' 'Eine vergessene Tradition – das Wesen der irischen Architektur' (1987) und 'Dublin – Baugeschichte einer Stadt' (1989). Die Liste realisierter Bauten umfaßt den Portikus des Abbey-Theaters, Dublin; den Umbau der 'Free Church', Dublin (Ford-Conservation-Preis 1990); die Vorlesungshalle für den Ingenieurverband, Dublin (AAI-Preis 1989).

———

Assistants / Assistenten – Brian Moran, Frank Cooney, Deirdre Kelly

Chapel of Reconciliation, Knock, Co Mayo (Competition, 1989)
Versöhnungskapelle in Knock (Wettbewerb 1989)

College Centre, Dublin (Invited Competition, 1991)
College-Zentrum in Dublin (Wettbewerb auf Einladung 1991)

Arranmore Island Housing (Competition 1990)
Wohnbauten auf der Arranmore-Insel (Wettbewerb 1990)

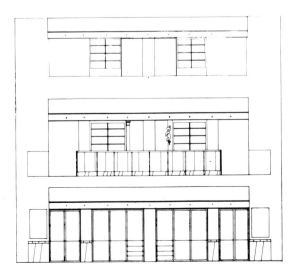

The Abbey Theatre Portico (1990)

The Portico for the Abbey Theatre in Dublin was designed to be in sympathy with the original facade, and yet stand in its own right as a piece of architecture, opening the building to the public realm and allowing the celebration of an evening at the theatre.

The Portico is intended as an architectural 'theatre' in itself, the stone centrepiece acting as a stage where the curved bar, canopy and balcony meet and are resolved in festive equilibrium. Externally, it was set in the context of a pedestrianised street, a Writer's Square for outdoor performances.

—

Der Portikus des 'Abbey'-Theaters (1990)

Der Portikus für das Dubliner 'Abbey'-Theater sollte mit der bestehenden Fassade des Theaters in Einklang stehen und gleichzeitig ein eigenständiges Stück Architektur darstellen, das das Gebäude für die Öffentlichkeit erschließt und das Feiern eines Abends im Theater ermöglioht. Der Portikus ist selbst ein architektonisches Theaterstück; sein Volumen aus Naturstein wirkt als Bühne, wo die geschwungene Bar, die leichte Decke und der Balkon zusammentreffen und sich in einem festlichen Gleichgewicht auflösen. Von außen sollte es in eine Fußgängerzone gesetzt sein, ein Schriftsteller-Platz für Aufführungen im Freien.

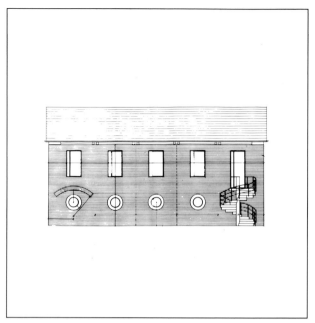

Institution of Engineers Lecture Hall (1989)

Taking up a garden plot behind a Victorian house, the Institution of Engineers Lecture Hall makes reference both to the typology of mews houses in the area and to Dublin tradition of lecture and meeting halls located at first floor level over an undercroft. The lecture hall is located over an archive room, with a staircase hall at one end.

Due to the narrowness of the site, the building depended for effect on its two main elevations: both are built in red brick laid in traditional Flemish bond. One is open with arcading towards the house, the other has a more closed aspect to the mews lane, its symmetric bank of windows offset by arches and a spiral staircase. (Architectural Association of Ireland Award, 1989).

Vorlesungshalle für den Ingenieur-Verband (1989)

Dieser Entwurf für das Gartengrundstück eines viktorianischen Hauses bezieht sich sowohl auf den Hinterhaus-Typus dieser Gegend als auch auf die für Dublin charakteristischen Vorlesungs- und Versammlungshallen, die im 1. Obergeschoß über den Deckengewölben des Erdgeschosses liegen. Diese Vorlesungshalle liegt über dem Archivraum, mit einem Treppenhaus in einem Hallenende.

Wegen des schmalen Grundstücks weist das Gebäude zwei besonders gestaltete Frontfassaden auf, die aus rotem Backstein-Mauerwerk im traditionell flämischen Backsteinverband errichtet wurden. Die Hoffassade ist offen gestaltet, während die Straßenfassade geschlossen wirkt. Die symmetrische Anordnung ihrer Fenster wird durch Bögen und eine Wendeltreppe ergänzt.
(Dieser Bau wurde 1989 mit dem 'Architectural Association of Ireland Award' ausgezeichnet.)

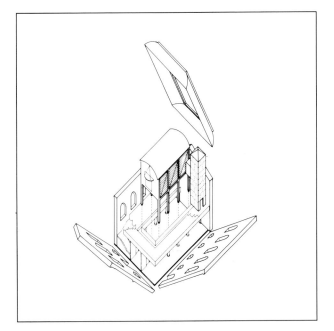

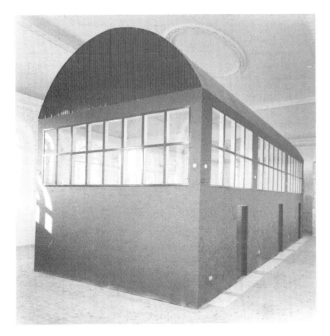

The Free Church (1989)

The Free Church, a Dublin Church of 1800, was adapted for use as a Travellers Centre. The intervention was concerned to maintain its original quality while making a definite statement of new use: this took the form of a complete 'house' within the church, a room on legs placed between the existing galleries to divide the space: the form of the old building remains untouched around it. The gallery level becomes a landscape of giant forms in paint and tin; the walls dividing rooms below are made from carefully dismantled timber pews. (Ford Conservation Award 1990).

Wolfman Jacks Restaurant (1989) *bottom-right*

The brief was to create a highly individual restaurant with 1950s ambience. The dining room was given shape by focussing on a raised dining platform in the centre, with more intimate booths under the shelter of aeroplane wings at both sides. The collision of elements with inclined columns created a tent-like carnival atmosphere.

Umbau der 'Free Church' (1989)

Die Dubliner 'Free Church', ein Sakralbau von 1800, wurde in ein Traveller-Zentrum umgebaut. Die ursprüngliche Substanz sollte bewahrt werden und die Neunutzung dennoch klar zum Ausdruck gebracht werden. Das Projekt nahm deshalb die Form eines in die Kirche gestellten 'Hauses' an. Dieses zwischen den Galerien aufgestellte 'Haus auf Beinen' unterteilt den Raum. Dadurch bleibt die ursprüngliche Form der Kirche unangetastet. Die Galerie-Ebene wird zu einer riesenhaften, farbig bemalten Blechlandschaft. Die Innenwände, die die Räume des Erdgeschosses unterteilen, sind aus den sorgfältig demontierten Kirchenbänken gefertigt worden. (Das Projekt wurde 1990 mit dem 'Ford Conservation Award' ausgezeichnet)

Wolfman Jacks Restaurant (1989) *unten rechts*

Durch einen im Stil der 50er Jahre geprägten Innenausbau sollte das Restaurant einen stark individuellen Charakter erhalten. Der Speisesaal enthält in der Saalmitte eine erhöhte Plattform mit Tischen, aber auch intimere Eßplätze unter dem Schutz von alten Flugzeugflügeln an beiden Seiten. Durch das Zusammentreffen verschiedener Elemente mit den geneigten Säulen wird eine Art Festzeltstimmung erzeugt.

McGARRY NíÉANAIGH ARCHITECTS

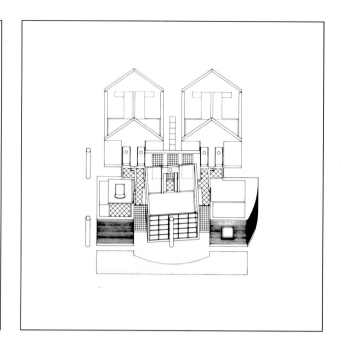

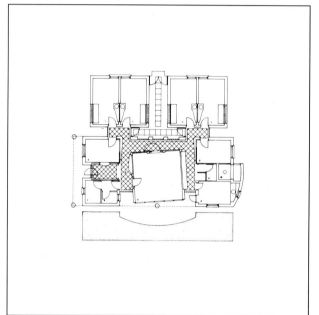

Michael McGarry – born in Dublin, 1955. Graduated from the School of Architecture, University College Dublin 1978. 1978-81: employed by Richard Rogers and Partners, London. Siobhan NíÉanaigh – born in Dublin, 1955. Graduated from School of Architecture, University College Dublin 1978. 1978-81: employed by de Blacam and Meagher, Dublin.

1981-1983: both principals employed by Josef Paul Kleihues in Rorup and Berlin and in the International Building Exhibition (IBA Berlin). Since 1984, both in private practice. Selected for exhibition in Architectural Association of Ireland's Awards exhibition every year since 1987 and AAI Award Winner 1991.

——

Michael McGarry wurde 1955 in Dublin geboren. Er promovierte an der Architekturfakultät des University College Dublin im Jahr 1978. Von 1978 bis 1981 arbeitete er im Architekturbüro Richard Rogers and Partners in London. Siobhan NíÉanaigh wurde 1955 in Dublin geboren. Sie promovierte an der Architekturfakultät des UCD im Jahr 1978. Von 1978 bis 1981 arbeitete sie im Architekturbüro von de Blacam & Meagher in Dublin. Von 1981 bis 1983 arbeiteten sie beide im Architekturbüro Josef Paul Kleihues in Rorup und Berlin und bei der Internationalen Bauausstellung Berlin. 1984 eröffneten sie zusammen ein Architekturbüro. Seit 1987 nehmen sie alljährlich an den AAI (der Irische Architekturverband) Wettbewerbsausstellungen teil. Im jahr 1991 gewannen sie einen AAI-Preis.

Collaborators and assistants / Mitarbeiter und Assistenten – Gerard Carthy, Peter Cody, Evelyn Duff, Paul Kelly, David Power

Medical Consulting Rooms (1990)

The building houses four doctors' consulting rooms in two blocks with secretarial and reception facilities in a third. The consulting rooms are to the north and rear of the building – their separate forms allowing a phased development of the scheme. The location is the outskirts of Drogheda – a town 50 km to the north of Dublin.

Accommodation in the main block includes entrance foyer, concourse, receptionist's office, waiting room for patients, toilets and secretarial offices. The concourse is arranged to avoid circulation cross-overs between patients coming to and from the consulting rooms. The waiting room faces south and is rotated relative to the building in deference to the main entrance and the exit route of patients leaving after consultation. The concourse is lit by a glass block wall with the waiting room reading as a freestanding object within it. The doctors' rooms have north light relieved by high-level east or west light over the examination couches. The doctors have a separate entrance from the rear of the building.

Praxis für eine Ärztegemeinschaft (1990)

Diese Gemeinschaftspraxis besteht aus vier Untersuchungsräumen, die in zwei gleichen Volumen untergebracht sind, sowie aus Empfangs- und Sekretariatsräumen in einem dritten Volumen. Die Untersuchungszimmer liegen im Norden auf der Rückseite des Häuserkomplexes. Ihre getrennten Formen erlauben eine Konstruktion in Phasen. Das Grundstück liegt in der Peripherie der 50 km nördlich von Dublin gelegenen Stadt Drogheda.

Im Hauptvolumen sind Empfangsraum und -büro, ein offener Durchgang, das Wartezimmer sowie WCs und Büros untergebracht. Die innere Erschließung zum Warteraum ist so organisiert, daß die ankommenden und die weggehenden Patienten sich nicht kreuzen. Das nach Süden orientierte Wartezimmer ist von der Gebäudeachse abgedreht, gegen den Haupteingang, und ist somit Ausdruck der 'Patientenzirkulation'. Das durch die Glasziegelwand des Korridors einfallende Licht läßt das Wartezimmer als ein allein stehendes Objekt erscheinen. Die Untersuchungsräume sind nach Norden ausgerichtet. Die Untersuchungsliegen sind unter Fenster plaziert, die nach Osten bzw. Westen hin orientiert sind. Die Ärzte haben einen separaten Eingang auf der Rückseite des Hauses.

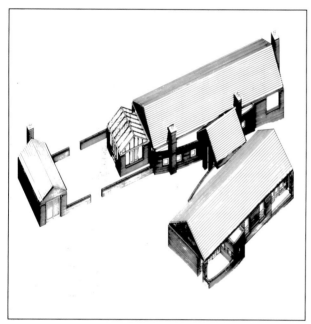
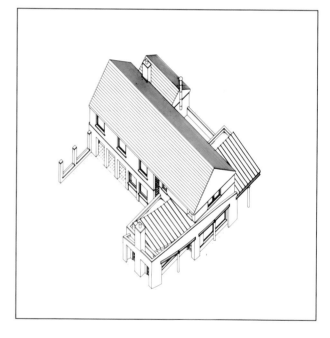

Brick House Facing the Mourne Mountains (1990) *left*

The program was for a family house on a very exposed north facing site with a spectacular view to the Mourne Mountains some 30 km away. The house is positioned in a meadow on the edge of the site in front of a newly planted copse. In order to maximise both the view and sunshine, the house is divided into three pieces – living wing facing west, bedroom wing facing east and an entrance building held between the two wings. Formally, the junction of the wings is handled by flat roofed curved secondary elements. The window aesthetic derives from the distinction between windows for viewing through and windows that can be opened.

House on the River Boyne (1991) *right*

The program was for a large family house on an elevated site on the north bank of the River Boyne estuary. An existing two-storey house on the site was gutted, reorientated, and extended towards the river. The ground floor is organised as a T-shaped plan with the principal living rooms stretched along the river elevation – the kitchen/living in the centre, the family and dining rooms at either end. Entrance to the house is along a collonade leading from the entrance yard at the west end. The main elevation is that to the river – the screen wall of the single storey elements is allowed to overlap on the gable of the main building.

Backstein-Wohnhaus gegen die Mourne Mountains (1990) *links*

Dieses Einfamilienhaus liegt auf einem sehr exponierten, nach Norden orientierten Grundstück und hat eine spektakuläre Aussicht auf die 30 KM entfernten Mourne Mountains. Es liegt am Rande des Grundstücks, inmitten einer Wiese und gegenüber einem aufgeforsteten Wäldchen. Um Aussicht und Sonneneinfall zu optimieren, ist das Haus in drei Teile gegliedert: einen nach Westen orientierten Wohntrakt, einen nach Osten orientierten Schlaftrakt und einen die beiden Flügel verbindenden Eingangsbau. Die formale Verbindung der Trakte wird durch geschwungene, flache Sekundärelemente hergestellt. Die Ästhetik der Fenster beruht auf ihren unterschiedlichen Funktionen: nur zum Hinausschauen oder aber zum Öffnen.

Haus am Boyne-Ufer (1991) *rechts*

Das erhöhte Grundstück dieses großen Einfamilienhauses liegt am nördlichen Ufer der Boyne-mündung. Ein bestehendes Haus wurde ausgekernt, neu strukturiert und zum Fluß hin erweitert. Der T-förmige Grundriß ist wie folgt organisiert: die Wohnräume sind parallel zum Flußufer, die Küche in der Hausmitte und das Eßzimmer und das Wohnungzimmer in denen äußersten teile des Gebäudes angelegt. Eine Kollonade führt vom Eingangshof zum Westende des Hauses. Eine durchgelöcherte Außenwand des eingeschossigen Körpers überschneidet sich mit der Giebelfassade des Hauptgebäudes.

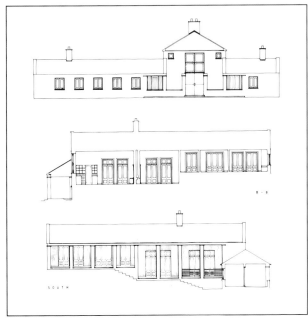
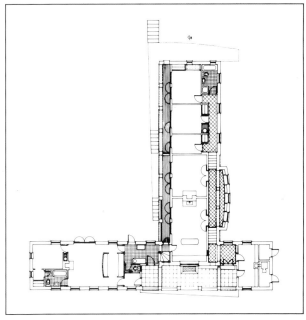

House on a Drumlin (1988)

This house is located in the north midlands of Ireland in a landscape of drumlins – a small ridged mound of glacial deposits. The program was for a farmhouse, a far office, and a separate apartment for the client's parent. The site slopes to the east – the gradient is 14%. The formal disposition of the scheme matches the program with the farmhouse running against the slope at right-angles to the parent's apartment and the farm office. The architectural problem of entrance is handled by forming an entrance court from which direct access is had to the farmhouse, the apartment, the farm office, and to a wash room. An orchard separates the building from the road. The farmhouse is organised such that all rooms face south and all have direct access to a loggia. The site section is used to divide the house into three levels (entrance, living, and bedrooms) with corresponding variation in ceiling heights. The circulation in the house similarly divides into three levels with a library recess at the living room level. The apartment is self-contained but is linked to the house through the wash room and the main kitchen.

Bauernhaus auf einem Hügel (1988)

Dieses Bauernhaus liegt inmitten einer Hügellandschaft von Gletscherablagerungen im nördlichen Mittelland Irlands. Der Entwurf sieht den Bau eines Bauernhauses, eines Büros sowie einer abgesonderten Wohnung für die Eltern des Bauherrn vor. Im Osten fällt das Grundstück um 14 % ab. Das Bauernhaus ist in den Hang hinein gebaut und steht in einem rechten Winkel zur Wohnung der Eltern und zum Büroteil. Durch einen gemeinsamen Vorplatz, von dem aus Bauernhaus, Wohnung, Büro und Waschküche zugänglich sind, wird das Eingangsproblem gelöst. Ein Obstgarten ist zwischen Haus und Straße angelegt. Durch die Ausrichtung des Hauses sind alle Räume nach Süden, gegen die Loggia, orientiert. Wegen der Hanglage des Grundstücks erfolgt die Raumabwicklung auf drei Ebenen; Eingang, Wohnen und Schlafen weisen verschiedene Raumhöhen auf. Die Zirkulation im Haus erfolgt in ähnlicher 3-Teilung mit einer Bibliotheksnische auf Wohnzimmer Ebene. Die Elternwohnung bildet eine geschlossene Einheit, ist aber durch Waschküche und Hauptküche mit dem Hauptgebäude verbunden.

O ' D O N N E L L   A N D   T U O M E Y
A R C H I T E C T S

Sheila O'Donnell and John Tuomey have worked independently on buildings, projects, post-graduate research and urban design since 1976. O'Donnell and Tuomey Architects was established in 1988. Current commissions include the Irish Film Centre, Temple Bar under construction 1991, and the Irish Pavilion at the 11 Cities/11 Nations exhibition, Netherlands 1990, re-erected in the Irish Museum of Modern Art, 1991. Studio lecturers at UCD and visiting professors at Princeton and Harvard; their work has been widely published and exhibited in Europe and America. They received AD Project Award 1984, Lord Mayor's Millennium Medal for Architecture 1988, AAI Awards 1986, 1987 and AAI Downes Medals 1988 and 1990.

———

Seit 1976 haben Sheila O'Donnell und John Tuomey unabhängig von einander an Gebauden, Projekten, Forschungsarbeiten nach beenoligter Studienzeit und Städteplanung gearbeitet. Das Architekturbüro O'Donnell and Tuomey wurde 1988 gegründet. In Auftragsarbeit entwarfen sie das Irische Filmzentrum das voraussichtlich 1991 realisiert wird, sowie den Irischen Pavillon für '11 Städte/11 Nationen' in den Niederlanden gezeigt und später im irischen 'Museum of Modern Art' wiederaufgebaut wird. Sie hielten Studio-Vorlesungen am UCD und waren Gastdozenten in Princeton und Harvard. Zahlreiche Arbeiten wurden in Europa und Amerika publiziert und ausgestellt. 1984 wurden sie mit einem AD-Projektpreis ausgezeichnet, 1988 die 'Millennium Medal', 1986 und 1987 weitere AAI-Auszeichnungen und 1988 und 1990 die 'AAI Downes Medal'.

Laboratory at Abbotstown (1985)
John Tuomey, Office of Public Works Dublin

Courthouse at Smithfield (1987)
John Tuomey, Office of Public Works Dublin

———

Laborgebäude in Abbotstown (1985)
Projekt von John Tuomey für das Hochbauamt Dublin

Gerichtsgebäude in Smithfield (1987)
Projekt von John Tuomey für das Hochbauamt Dublin

Assistants / Assistenten – Sean Mahon, Marcus Donaghy, Emma O'Neill, Susan Cogan, Esmonde O'Briain, Jens Kuchermeister, Tom Power

Irish Pavilion (1990)

An Artist – Architect Collaboration
11 Cities / 11 Nations Exhibition, Netherlands, 1990
Irish Museum of Modern Art, 1991

The architectural design responds to the content of Brian Maguire's recent paintings which deal principally with closed institutions (prison) and personal relationships (love). Common ground between architects and artist was found in discussion of Beckett's writings, which had inspired some of the paintings. The timber and corrugated iron building contains elements such as ladders and catwalks which intensify the experience of viewing each particular picture.

Irischer Pavillon (1990)

Ein Gemeinschaftsprojekt zwischen dem Maler und den Architekten für die '11 Städte / 11 Nationen-Ausstellung' in den Niederlanden, 1990 Wiederaufbau im Irischen Museum für Moderne Kunst, 1991

Der Entwurf nimmt auf die neuesten Bilder von Brian Maguire Bezug, die sich inhaltlich um geschlossene Institutionen (Gefängnis) und zwischenmenschliche Beziehungen (Liebe) drehen. Einen gemeinsamen Anknüpfungspunkt fanden Künstler und Architekten in enden Werk von Samuel Beckett, die den Maler zu einigen Bildern inspirierten. Im Innern des wellblechverkleideten Pavillons aus Holzkonstruktion wird durch Elemente wie Stufenleitern und Laufstege der Eindruck des gesonderten Betrachtens jedes einzelnen Bildes noch verstärkt.

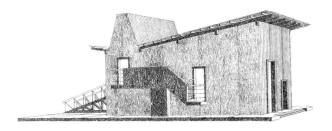

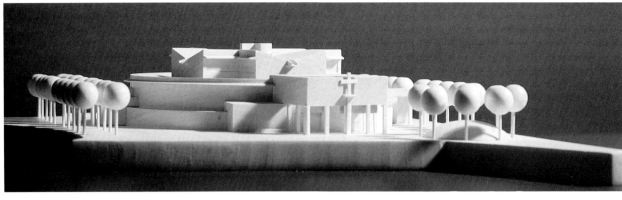

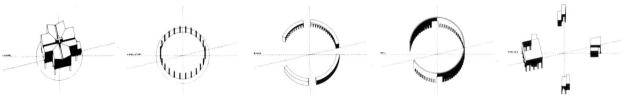

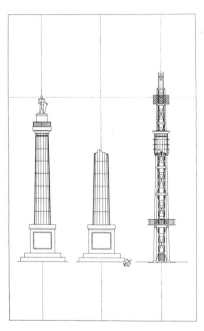

Chapel of Reconciliation (1988)
Competition Entry, Knock

A circular floor plan unites the ambulatory, for preparation and access to the reconciliation boxes for 300 penitents and the church for 500. The 'ring' (ambulatory) and the 'cross' (church) are expressed externally by sloping metal sheeted roofs and internally by daylight provided through clerestory glazing. The contemplative character of the space is modulated by the variety of the ceiling heights, the parallax of the steel and concrete columns, and the quality of the light throughout the chapel.

The Pillar Project (1988)
Artist – Architect Collaboration: Felim Egan – O'Donnell and Tuomey

The Nelson Monument in O'Connell Street, Dublin's main street, was built in 1808 to celebrate the British victory at Trafalgar, but its intended symbolism had been translated over time into the collective culture. It was a landmark defining the city centre, a terminus for public transport and a popular meeting place. Despite the removal of 'The Pillar' in 1966 its memory persists, giving it a presence in the public consciousness which contradicts the evidence of the void. This project reinstates some strategic elements of the monument, giving them a new role at their original location on the site.

Die Versöhnungskapelle (1988)

Der kreisförmige Grundriß vereinigt einen Wandelgang im äußeren Ring, in dem Beichtstühle für 300 Personen aufgereiht sind, und von dem aus auch der 500 Personen fassende Kirchenraum zugänglich ist. Der Ring des Wandelganges und die Kreuzform der Kirche kommen außen in Form geneigter Blechdächer und innen durch den Tageslichteinfall der Oberlichtfenster zum Ausdruck. Der kontemplative Charakter des Raumes entsteht durch die verschiedenen Raumhöhen, die Parallelachse der Stahl- und Betonsäulen sowie das gestreute Licht.

Das Säulen-Projekt (1988)
Ein Gemeinschaftsprojekt zwischen dem Künstler Felim Egan und den Architekten O'Donnell & Tuomey

Das Nelson-Monument an Dublins Hauptstraße O'Connell Street wurde 1808 errichtet, um des britischen Sieges in Trafalgar zu gedenken; aber die beabsichtigte Symbolik wurde im Laufe der Zeit in eine kollektive Kultur übersetzt. Dieses Wahrzeichen des Stadtzentrums war Endstation des öffentlichen Verkehrs und ein beliebter Treffpunkt gewesen. Trotz der gewaltsamen Entfernung im Jahr 1966 hat sich die Erinnerung daran im öffentlichen Bewußtsein bewahrt, was der Offensichtlichkeit der Lücke widerspricht.
Das Projekt setzt einige strategische Elemente der alten Säule wieder ein, schreibt ihnen aber eine neue Rolle am alten Standort zu.

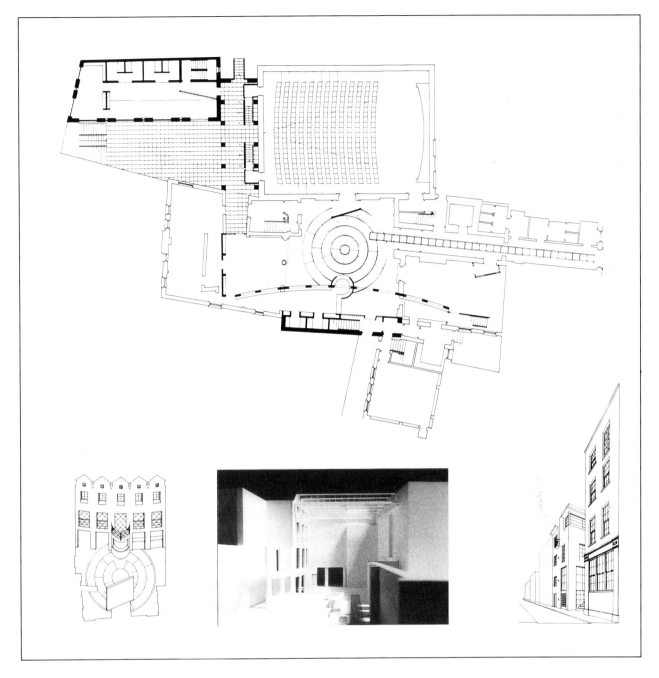

Irish Film Centre, Temple Bar (construction 1991)

The Film Centre will occupy the former Quakers Headquarters, a remarkable assemblage of buildings accumulated since 1692. It is at the centre of a city block with no significant street frontage, but narrow routes of access from three streets. The building will accommodate all aspects of film culture, including two cinemas, a film archive, a restaurant, bar and offices.

Three sides of a new glass roofed courtyard are formed by existing buildings, on the fourth side a new building, with its wall gently curved like a lens, houses offices, bar and information/sales.

The new archive building in smooth brick with steel window forms an external public courtyard with steps down to Sycamore Street.

In general new elements are treated as installations, standing in contrast to the existing buildings and combining with it to create a lively environment for the viewing and discussion of film.

Irisches Filmzentrum, Temple-Bar (realisation 1991)

Das Filmzentrum belegt das Areal des frühereh Quäker-Zentrums, eine bemerkenswerte Ansammlung von Häusern, die bis auf das Jahr 1692 zurückgehen. Es liegt im Hof einer Blockrandbebauung, die nur über drei schmale Zufahrtswege verfügt. Das Filmzentrum bietet Raum für zwei Kinos, ein Film-Archiv, ein Restaurant, eine Bar und Büroräume.

Drei Seiten des glasüberdachten Innenhofes werden von bestehenden Häusern begrenzt; die vierte Seite bildet eine leicht geschwungene Wand eines Neubaus. In diesem Teil sind Büros, Bar, Information und Verkauf untergebracht.

Die Längsfassade des neuen Archivgebäudes mit dem glatten Backstein-Mauerwerk und den Stahlfenstern bildet gegen die Sycamore Street einen durch Freitreppen erreichbaren öffentlichen Außenhof.

Im allgemeinen werden die Einzelvolumen des Neubaus als 'Installationen' behandelt, die sich mit den bestehenden Gebäuden ergänzen oder damit kontrastieren. So wird eine anregende Umgebung für den Kinobesuch geschaffen.

SHANE O'TOOLE
ARCHITECT

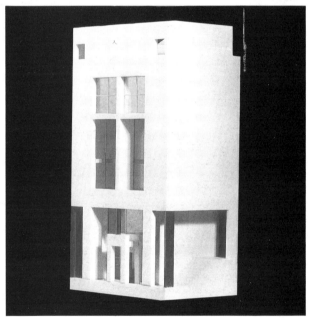

Born in Dublin in 1955, he graduated from UCD in 1979. He was President of the Architectural Association of Ireland in 1982/83 and Vice President of the Royal Institute of the Architects of Ireland in 1988. An editor of many architectural publications, he works at UCD, where he has for several years managed European R & D projects aimed at promoting the rational use of energy in buildings.

Winner of the Grand Prix at the 1989 Cracow Biennale, he is now a Trustee of the Architecture Academy Foundation in that city. He was the sole Irish participant in the RIBA's 1988 exhibition, '40 Under 40: Young Architects in Britain', and is a laureate of 'Interarch'.

———

Er wurde 1955 in Dublin geboren. 1979 promovierte er am University College in Dublin. 1982/83 war er Präsident des irischen Architektenverbandes (Architectural Association of Ireland) und 1988 Vize-Präsident des 'Royal Institute of the Architects of Ireland'. Als Herausgeber von vielen Architekturpublikationen ist er heute am University College in Dublin beschäftigt, wo er auch während mehreren Jahren Forschungs- und Entwicklungsprojekte der EG für energiesparendes Bauen leitete.

An der Krakauer Biennale 1989 gewann er den ersten Preis. Heute ist er Kurator der 'Architecture Academy Foundation' in Krakau. 1988 nahm er als einziger irischer Architekt an der RIBA-Ausstellung '40 unter 40' teil und wurde Preisträger an der 'Interarch'.

The Making of a Modern Street, Dublin (1980)
Michael Kelly and Shane O'Toole

The project reinterprets the typical Dublin Georgian plot and explores the urban qualities it offers. The design was presented for public exhibition in the manner of James Malton's views of 18th-century Dublin. The chosen view is of the gallery which hosted that exhibition, which was originated by Michael de Courcy.

Bau einer modernen Straße, Dublin (1980)
Michael Kelly und Shane O'Toole

Das Projekt findet eine neue Interpretation für das, für Dublin so typische, georgianische Grundstück und erforscht die städtischen Qualitäten, die es bietet. Der Plan wurde für eine öffentliche Ausstellung präsentiert und zwar in Form von James Malton's 'Ansichten von Dublin im 18. Jahrhundert'. Die Wahl fiel auf die Ansicht der Galerie, in der die Ausstellung, die Michael de Courcy initiierte, stattfand.

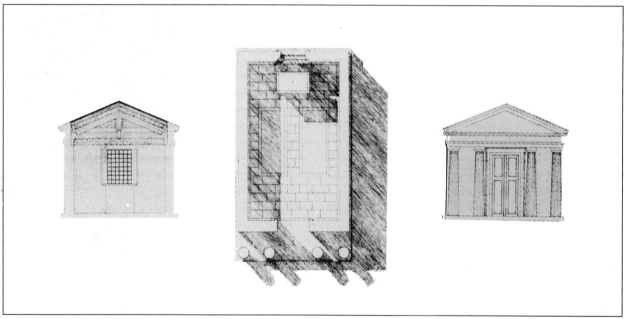

Papal Altar, Killeneer, Drogheda, Co Louth (1979)
Lynch O'Toole Walsh (James O'Toole and Shane O'Toole, with Michael de Courcy) and Turlough McKevitt [photo:RTE Film & Illustrations Library]

Von Rohr Mausoleum, Newstown, Co Carlow (1986)
Lynch O'Toole Walsh (James O'Toole and Shane O'Toole)

These are the first and last projects I designed with my father: sacred objects rising out of the land. The Papal Altar, seen by 500 million people world-wide, existed no more than a few fleeting hours. Nothing endures. Nothing can escape the shadow of latent decay, not even a carefully proportioned sepulchre of fine material... The cattle return to graze.

Päpstlicher Altar, Killeneer, Drogheda (Louth) 1979
Lynch O'Toole Walsh (James O'Toole und Shane O'Toole, mit Michael de Courcy) und Turlough McKevitt

Von Rohr Mausoleum, Newstown (Carlow) 1986
Lynch O'Toole Walsh (James O'Toole und Shane O'Toole)

Dies sind meine ersten und letzten Projekte, die ich zusammen mit meinem Vater entwarf: Geweihte Objekte, die aus der Landschaft herausragen. Der päpstliche Altar, der von über 500 Millionen Menschen auf der ganzen Welt gesehen wurde, existierte nur gerade ein paar flüchtige Stunden lang. Nichts hat Bestand. Nichts kann dem Schatten des allgegenwärtigen Zerfalls entkommen, nicht einmal ein sorgfältig proportioniertes Grabmal aus feinsten Materialien... Die Kühe kehren zurück auf die Weide, um zu grasen.

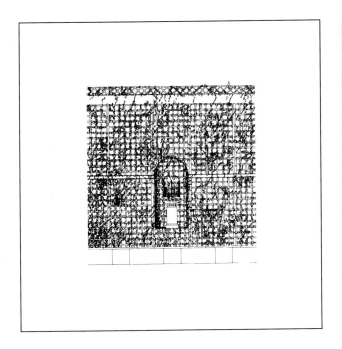

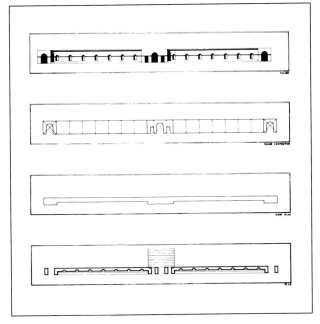

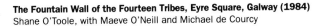

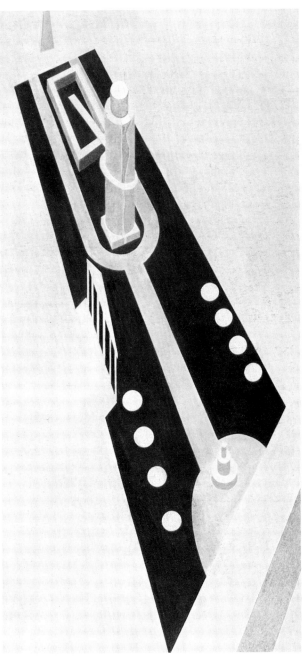

The Fountain Wall of the Fourteen Tribes, Eyre Square, Galway (1984)
Shane O'Toole, with Maeve O'Neill and Michael de Courcy

The Pillar Project, O'Connell Street, Dublin (1988)
Shane O'Toole, Leo Higgins and James Scanlon, with Niamh Butler

It is the role of monuments, located in the great public outdoor
rooms, through speculative enquiry to interpret and give form to the
memories of cities. Overgrown with ivy, a green wall in a grey square
evokes familiar images of ruined buildings, of the fourteen towers and
gates of the mediaeval city wall. The Pillar, traumatically destroyed a
generation ago, returns, transformed: from the fissure in its ruptured
shell, a chrysalis emerging, stained glass glowing, a great new
metropolitan secular cathedral; the citizen restored to his abacus, the
viewing point of an ideal observer of the city.

*During the Dublin Millennium in 1988, Shane O'Toole coordinated the
award-winning 'Pillar Project', in which architects and artists
collaborated on proposals for a replacement for Dublin's symbol – the
Nelson Pillar – blown up 25 years ago.*

Mauer mit Springbrunnen für die vierzehn Stämme, Galway (1984)
Shane O'Toole mit Maeve O'Neill und Michael de Courcy

Das Säulen Projekt, Dublin (1988)
Shane O'Toole, Leo Higgins und James Scanlon, mit Niamh Butler

Es ist die Aufgabe der Monumente, die in großen öffentlichen Anlagen
stehen, die Erinnerungen einer Stadt durch spekulative
Nachforschungen zu interpretieren und ihnen Form zu geben. Eine
grüne, von Efeu überwucherte Mauer auf einem grauen Platz ruft
vertraute Bilder von zerfallenen Gebäuden, von den vierzehn Türmen
und Toren der mittelalterlichen Stadtmauer, hervor. Die Nelson-Säule
– vor einer Generation auf traumatische Art und Weise zerstört –
kehrt durch dieses Projekt verwandelt zurück: aus dem Spalt der
aufgebrochenen Schale, kommt die Puppe zum Vorschein;buntes Glas
lwuchtet, eine großartige neue säkulare Kathedrale der Hauptstadt:
der Bärger ist seiner Säule wiedergegeben, der Aussichtspunkt eines
idealen Beobachters der Stadt.

*Im Rahmen der Dubliner 1000-Jahr-Feier koordinierte Shane O'Toole
das 'Säulenprojekt', ein Gemeinschaftsprojekt von Architekten und
Künstlern, die Vorschläge für eine neue Nelson-Säule – das vor 25
Jahren in die Luft gesprengte Symbol von Dublin – ausarbeiteten.*

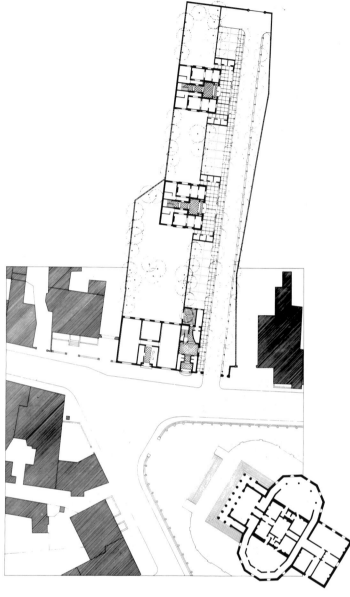

DEREK TYNAN ARCHITECTS

Derek Tynan graduated from UCD in 1977 and from Cornell University with a Masters of Architecture (Urban Design) in 1982. He worked with Rick Mather Architects, London, and Cleary + Hall, Dublin, before establishing his own practice. He has taught in various Architecture schools, most recently in UCD and the University of Virginia. Projects and buildings have been published and exhibited in Ireland, Europe and the USA. Was a founder member of the City Architecture Studio and a contributor to *Projects for the Liffey Quays*, 1984. As head of Urban Design Unit, NBA 1986-89 was responsible for preparation of urban design proposals including Wexford – North End, and Galway – Spanish Arch.

——

Derek Tynan promovierte 1977 am University College Dublin und erhielt 1982 ein 'Master Degree' für Architektur und Städtebau von der Cornell University. Er arbeitete im Büro der Rick Mather Architects in London sowie bei Cleary + Hall in Dublin, bevor er sein eigenes Büro eröffnete. Er unterrichtete an mehreren Universitäten, seit kurzem am University College in Dublin, und an der 'University of Virginia'. Seine Bauten und Projekte wurden in Irland, Europa und den USA publiziert und ausgestellt. Er war Gründungsmitglied des 'City Architecture Studio' und Mitarbeiter bei den 'Projekten für die Liffey-Kais' 1984. Als Leiter der Städtebau-Abteilung bei der Nationalen Bauagentun von 1986-89 war er für verschiedene städtebauliche Projekte verantwortlich, u.a. für die Erneuerungsprojekte für Wexford – North End und für das 'Spanish Arch'-Gelände in Galway.

Assistants / Assistenten – Vivienne Brophy, John Dorman, Eoin St John Downes, James Doyle, David Kelly, Esmond O'Brian, Eilis O'Donnell, Antoinette O'Neill, Emma O'Neill, Tom Power, Mel Reynolds

NBA Urban Design Unit – MB O'Connor CTO, Reenie Elliott, Michael McShane, Una Sugrue

Apartment and Office Building, Carlow (1986)

Redefining a triangular space opposite William Vitruvius Morrison's courthouse, this project was concerned with the re-establishment of a mixed use building type. Fronting on to the urban space is a building with ground floor offices with apartments above. Entered through a gateway, formed as a continuation of the street facade, is a tree-lined avenue with two further apartment buildings, conceived as urban villas.

Büro-/Wohnhaus in Carlow (1986)

Dieser Entwurf befaßte sich mit dem Neubau eines Büro-/Wohnhauses, der das gegenübeliegende, dreieckige Grundstück mit dem Morrison's Gerichtsgebäude neu definieren sollte. Das Erdgeschoß wird für Büros, die Obergeschosse für Wohnungen genutzt. Das Gebäude ist durch ein Tor, die Straßenfassade fortsetzend, die mit einer Baumallee bepflanzt ist, erreichbar. Entlang der Baumallee sind zwei weitere Wohnhäuser, eine Art städtische Villen, errichtet worden.

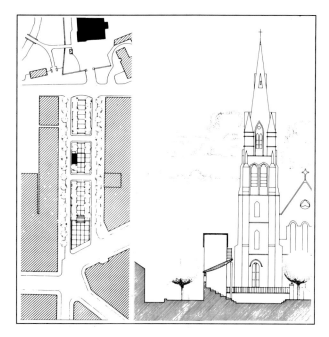

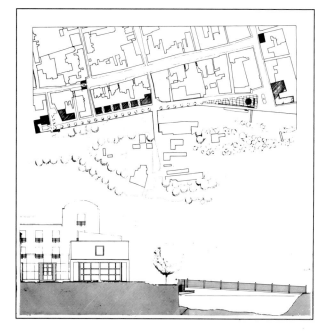

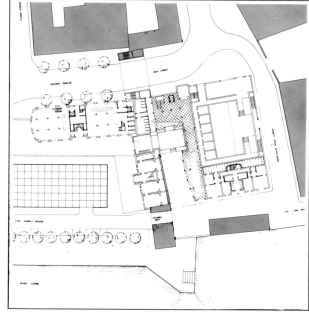

St Michael's Square, Ballinasloe (1989) *top-left*
NBA Urban Design Unit / Derek Tynan, Head of Unit

A project for the restructuring of the main urban space of the town. Elements of a civic architecture are recombined to form a central definition within the linear space.

Suir Quays, Clonmel (1990) *bottom-left*

As part of a larger urban design project, a proposal for the definition of a new urban edge to the town. Included is the restructuring of Old Quay to provide a new pedestrian sequence from town to park and a visitors centre as a public monument.

Municipal Theatre, Galway (1987) *right*
NBA Urban Design Unit / Derek Tynan, Head of Unit

A proposal for the rebuilding of the historic area of Spanish Arch, with fragments of the medieval town wall and 19th century buildings retained. The line of the town wall is redefined and the existing Fishmarket Square remade, with the theatre — located outside the original wall — axially related through a public room in the thickness of the wall. The scale of the theatre is contained by smaller elements which accommodate it to the periphery of the site.

St Michael's Square in Ballinasloe (1989) *oben links*

Es handelt sich um ein Erneuerungsprojekt für den wichtigsten Platz der Stadt. Elemente der öffentlichen Architektursprache werden so kombiniert, daß sie einen zentralen Bezugspunkt innerhalb des linearen Platzes bilden.

Suir Quays, Clonmel (1990) *unten links*

Dieser Vorschlag, der Bestandteil eines umfassenden städtebaulichen Projektes ist, befaßt sich mit der Definierung eines neuen Stadtrandes. Der 'Old Quay' wird neu strukturiert und sieht eine neue Fußgängerzone von der Stadt bis zum Park vor und beinhaltet auch ein Besucherzentrum als öffentliches Monument.

Stadttheater in Galway (1987) *rechts*

In diesem Erneuerungsvorschlag für 'Spanish Arch' werden Fragmente der mittelalterlichen Stadtmauer und Bauten aus dem 19. Jahrhundert erhalten. Der Verlauf der Stadtmauer wird neu definiert und der Platz des Fischmarktes erneuert. Das außerhalb der Stadtmauer gelegene Theater wird durch einen, die Mauer fortsetzenden, öffentlich genutzten Raum axial verbunden. Der Maßstab des Theatergebäudes wird durch kleinere Elemente dem Maßstab der Umgebung angepaßt.

D O U B L E   H O U S E
BELGRAVE SQUARE MONKSTOWN

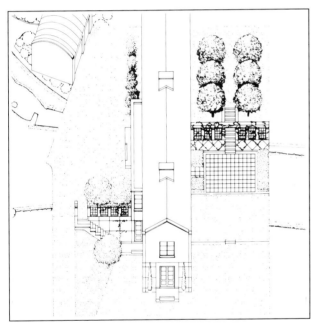

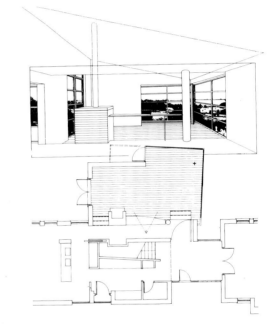

House at Athy, Co Kildare (1988) *left*

Located in the undulating landscape of the Barrow Valley, this design was concerned with its placement within, and as part of the landscape. Reference is made to the long house typology of adjacent houses and barns, differentiating between a clear external form and an internal spatial complexity. Entrance is on the upper level, and a sequence is developed through which both the house and landscape unfold leading to the family living areas on the lower levels.

Double House, Monkstown, Co Dublin (1989) *top-right*

A project for two dwellings as an attachment to an end-of-terrace Regency house, itself to be refurbished into six apartments. The two houses are considered as a single attachment or mews to the main house, expressed as a single gable.

House at Ballitore, Co Kildare (1990) *bottom-right*

A project for a house with associated stables on the periphery of a town, containing a walled burial ground. The project is conceived as a further farm settlement with a distinct geometry, the primary volume of the house reading as a figure onto which specific pieces, engaging programme and landscape, are accreted.

Carbery-Einfamilienhaus in Athy (Kildare) 1988 *links*

Die Ausrichtung des Hauses innerhalb der hügeligen Landschaft des Barrow Valley war Ausgangspunkt des Entwurfs. Das Gebäude nimmt auf die Langhaustypologie der umliegenden Häuser und Scheunen Bezug. Die klare äußere Form unterscheidet sich von einer komplexen inneren Räumlichkeit. Es wird eine Reihenfolge entwickelt, durch die sich Haus und die Landschaft entfalten, und zu den Wohnräumen in den unteren Ebenen führen.

Doppelhaus in Monkstown (Dublin) 1989 *oben rechts*

Die projektierte Erweiterung eines bestehenden, im Regentenstil erbauten Wohnhauses soll sechs Wohnungen enthalten. Der langgezogene Baukörper mit einem Giebeldach wird als Hinterhaus des Hauptgebäudes betrachtet.

Bauernhof in Ballitore (Kildare) 1990 *unten rechts*
In den Entwurf für einen Bauernhof mit Stallgebäuden, die klare Geometrie des Hauses hebt sich deutlich von der umgebenden Landschaft ab. Das Hauptvolumen kann als eine Gestalt gelesen werden, auf die besondere Teile, Programm und Landschaft bezogen sind.

SHAY CLEARY ARCHITECTS

18 Palmerston Park, Dublin 6
tel 01-96662 / fax 973053

GRAFTON ARCHITECTS

97 Grafton Street, Dublin 2
tel 01-713365 / fax 713178

PAUL KEOGH ARCHITECTS

1 Johnson Place, Dublin 2
tel 01-6791551 / fax 6793476

McCULLOUGH MULVIN ARCHITECTS

29 South Anne Street, Dublin 2
tel 01-6798019 / fax 6798137

McGARRY NíÉANAIGH ARCHITECTS

21 Laurence Street, Drogheda
tel 041-32297 / fax 36009

O'DONNELL AND TUOMEY ARCHITECTS

20 Camden Row, Dublin 8
tel 01-537200 / fax 751479

SHANE O'TOOLE ARCHITECT

68 Irishtown Road, Dublin 4
tel 01-609843

DEREK TYNAN ARCHITECTS

27 Lower Camden Street, Dublin 2
tel 01-751130 / fax 783636

MAKING A MODERN STREET

AN URBAN PROPOSAL – THE WORK OF 8 IRISH ARCHITECTS

BAU EINER MODERNEN STRAßE

EIN STÄDTEBAU ENTWURF – DIE ARBEIT VON 8 IRISCHEN ARCHITEKTEN